D0323876

THE AMERICAN NEGRO
HIS HISTORY AND LITERATURE

NEGRO NEWCOMERS
IN DETROIT

George Edmund Haynes

*

THE NEGRO
IN WASHINGTON

Prepared by the Federal Writers Project

ARNO PRESS and THE NEW YORK TIMES
NEW YORK 1969

Reprint edition 1969 by Arno Press, Inc.
Introduction copyright © 1969 by Arno Press, Inc.
All rights reserved

*

Library of Congress Catalog Card No. 76–94132

*

The Negro in Washington originally appeared in Washington: City and Capital,
American Guide Series, Federal Writers' Project, and is reprinted from
a copy in The State Historical Society of Wisconsin Library

*

Manufactured in the United States of America

General Editor
WILLIAM LOREN KATZ

F
574
.D4
H3

Cumberland (doc. Sci) Univ 9/8/71 NY.

OVER THE PAST HALF-CENTURY, AFRO-AMERICAN LIFE HAS been transformed by the exodus of hundreds of thousands of black people from the farms and small towns of the South to the major cities of the border states, the North, and the West. Beginning in the World War I period, this great migration has changed black Americans from a fundamentally rural to a largely urban people and has had an impact on American cities—and indeed on all of American society—that has not yet been fully assessed. The two pieces in this volume are documents of this social and geographic transformation. George Edmund Haynes's pamphlet, *Negro New-Comers in Detroit,* comes out of the initial phase of the migration, during the World War I years. Sterling Brown's *The Negro in Washington,* a chapter from a WPA Federal Writers' Project guidebook to the nation's capitol, *Washington: City and Capitol,* is a brief sketch of black life in a border city after a generation of large scale migration.

The Haynes pamphlet, published in 1918, was a contemporary survey of social conditions among blacks in Detroit, which had become a major destination for the World War I migrants. Before the war, the black population of the United States had been overwhelmingly southern and rural—less than 10% lived in the North. New York, Chicago and Philadelphia had well-established, although still small, black communities,

BALLOU LIBRARY
BUENA VISTA COLLEGE
STORM LAKE, IOWA 50588

90811

but less than 6,000 Afro-Americans lived in Detroit in 1910. Detroit's black population increased by over 600% in the next decade, and the influx of thousands of black people— mostly impoverished and uneducated—into a city that had been almost entirely white, created a wide range of new social problems. The migration did not create the ghetto; even before the war, white discrimination had forced blacks into segregated residential districts. But it did strain the facilities of black Detroit, generating problems of overcrowding, family disorganization, poverty and disease. And it brought to the surface white animosities that had previously been submerged.

In addition to its survey of living conditions in the city, *Negro New-Comers in Detroit* recommends various social action programs to religious organizations. It is a classic document of progressive reform, of the belief that the study of social problems, followed by a program of education and uplift, could substantially ameliorate the ills of society.

Haynes was one of the first back Americans to be professionally trained as a sociologist. Born in Arkansas in 1880, he attended Fisk, Yale and the University of Chicago, and received his Ph.D. from Columbia in 1910. His doctoral dissertation, *The Negro at Work in New York City,* was published in 1912. Like most sociologists of his generation, Haynes regarded his writings as blueprints for social change, and was as much an activist as he was a scholar. One of the founders of the National Urban League in 1910, he also held positions with the YMCA and the Interworld Church Movement, and during World War I he took leave from his teaching post at Fisk to serve as Director of Negro Economics for the U.S. Department of Labor.

Haynes's analysis is sober in its appraisal of existing conditions, sanguine in its prognosis for the future. Despite the full employment offered in the war years, Haynes recognized the difficulties that black workers would face in holding on to their gains after the war. Yet he saw this problem not primarily as a function of white discrimination but as the result of the poor training and bad working habits of the black labor force. He believed that blacks needed only to do "the work open to them with such efficiency and satisfaction that . . . their labor will be wanted along with that of other labor groups." He realistically assessed the overcrowding, high rents and poor facilities in the burgeoning black ghetto and recognized that segregation in housing had existed even before the wartime influx. Yet his solutions are piecemeal— model apartments, more playgrounds, additional sociological studies. He perceived the social ills spawned by the ghetto —poverty, crime, delinquency, alcoholism—but offered as palliatives community dances and wholesome motion pictures. In short, Haynes's analysis is in the tradition of Booker T. Washington's philosophy of self-help and racial uplift. He eschewed the militant protest of W. E. B. Du Bois and the young but vigorous National Association for the Advancement of Colored People, and emphasized instead the need for education, volunteer programs and mutual cooperation. The prospect for a better future, he believed, lay in the realization of the "spirit of Christ"—a spirit that white Detroiters, and white Americans in general, were to keep well-concealed for many years to come.

The Negro in Washington, written almost twenty years later, reflects a wholly different spirit. The harsh realities of ghetto life in the Twenties and, most important, the desperate economic plight of black people during the Great Depression, had destroyed the genial reformism of George Haynes's generation. Booker T. Washington's program of self-help had long since lost popular favor, and the NAACP's militant liberalism now vied with more radical ideologies for the support of a new generation of black Americans. The young black writers who compiled this article under the direction of Sterling Brown were victims of the massive unemployment of the Great Depression and they present a blunt, straight-forward account of Afro-American life in the capitol city during the economic crisis.

The Negro in Washington is both history and contemporary analysis. The history is remarkably good—concise and sympathetic. Unlike much of the Afro-American history of its day, it does not concern itself merely with white attitudes and policies toward blacks; instead it focuses on the activities of black Washingtonians themselves. It treats Washington's history as part of the nation's history, but also recognizes the capitol's peculiarities. It points to Washington's split personality, being both a northern and a southern city, straddling the Mason and Dixon Line. It assesses the impact of Washington's virtual lack of industry on black economic life and provides a vivid portrait of a unique aspect of the city's social pathology—its "alley-dwelling" problem.

The contemporary analysis is remarkably free of sugar coating or false optimism, documenting the discrimination, poverty and police brutality faced daily by Afro-Americans in Washington. The authors, themselves the beneficiaries of New Deal social welfarism, credit the Roosevelt administration with some achievements in relieving the economic plight of black Washington, but they find that it had done little to crack the racism of the whites or the political apathy of the blacks. Their conclusions are not comforting. Separate but not equal, still the order of the day in Washington, really means separate and unequal, and much remains to be done before black people can enjoy the full rights of citizenship in their own capitol.

Although different in approach and emphasis, these two selections are linked by a common concern with black migration in twentieth century urban America. Examining different cities at different times and from different perspectives, they provide brief yet incisive glimpses of modern America's greatest unsolved social problem.

Allan H. Spear
DEPARTMENT OF HISTORY
UNIVERSITY OF MINNESOTA

NEGRO NEWCOMERS
IN DETROIT

George Edmund Haynes

NEGRO NEW-COMERS

IN

DETROIT, MICHIGAN

A Challenge to Christian Statesmanship

A Preliminary Survey

By

GEORGE EDMUND HAYNES, Ph.D.

Professor of Social Science, Fisk University; Educational
Secretary, National League on Urban Conditions
Among Negroes; Director of Negro Economics,
Department of Labor.

HOME MISSIONS COUNCIL
156 Fifth Avenue
New York

1918

HOME MISSIONS COUNCIL

COMMITTEE ON NEGRO WORK

Rev. S. L. Morris, Chairman, Atlanta, Georgia

Rev. Dr. H. Paul Douglass,   Rev. Gilbert N. Brink.

Rev. Dr. C. L. White,   Rev. Dr. John M. Moore,

Survey of Detroit's Negro Population

At the annual meeting of the Home Missions Council, held in New York City, January 15-17, 1918, the results of a careful survey of Negro conditions in Detroit, Michigan, which had been made by Professor George E. Haynes of Fisk University, Nashville, Tenn., were presented, and a summary was embodied in the Annual Report. In response to a request for wider circulation this print of the Survey in full is issued. Since the Survey was made, Dr. Haynes has become Director of Negro Economics in the Department of Labor, Washington, D. C.

Detroit was selected because of the large numbers of negroes, who have been attracted to that city; and also because it is believed that the conditions in Detroit, although changing, are sufficiently typical of other northern, industrial centers as to give a fairly accurate understanding of this modern phase of the negro problem, which may have acute and serious aspects if not speedily cared for by an enlightened judgment, and the quickened conscience of the Christian church.

ALFRED WILLIAMS ANTHONY,

Executive Secretary.

3

PREFATORY NOTE

At the beginning of this survey the investigator wishes to emphasize its preliminary character. Having had a very short time to gather the material and to analyze and work it up, he is painfully conscious of the danger of snapshot vision and hasty inferences. A more complete body of facts and opinions might greatly alter the indications stated in the pages which follow. The inferences and recommendations must, therefore, be taken with this fact in mind.

The methods have been those usually pursued by careful students. Much of the statistical data had already been gathered by Mr. Forrester B. Washington, the efficient director of the Detroit League on Urban Conditions Among Negroes, or under his personal supervision. It is a pleasure to give expression of my thanks to him for his many courtesies in this connection. My gratitude is due also to many others; ministers, laymen and social workers who so cordially furnished me with facts and opinions.

GEORGE E. HAYNES

Nashville, Tenn.,
    March 12, 1918.

TABLE OF CONTENTS:

CHAPTER I.

Introduction
  1. The General Migration.
  2. New-comers to Detroit, Michigan.

CHAPTER II.

The Industrial Opportunity.

CHAPTER III.

Housing and Recreation of New-comers.

CHAPTER IV.

The Church and the People.

CHAPTER V.

General Summary and Recommendations.

CHAPTER I.

Introduction

I.—THE GENERAL MIGRATION

During the past two years large numbers of Negroes from the border and Southern states have migrated to the North and settled mainly in the industrial centers.

The general estimate of the number of Negroes who have left the South during the past two years is from 300,000 to more than 500,000. The latter figure is probably not an exaggeration as near as a numerical estimate of the movement can now be made based upon statements of observers, the records of insurance companies, of railway ticket offices and from other sources.

The Economic Cause of Migration

This migration is only the third swell in a movement of Negroes to the cities and to the North which has been in progress since 1860. The manner and causes have been the same. The movement was greatly increased between 1870 and 1880 and between 1890 and 1900 in a similar way though in smaller proportions than the present migration. Basing his judgment upon census figures and reliable information secured largely through repeated visits to rural and urban districts of the southern states the writer concludes that the cause first in importance in the present migration is economic. Those districts in the South that suffered most during the past four years, from the low price of cotton, from the boll-weevil, from floods and droughts consequently have had the worse economic conditions to face and thus have lost largest numbers of their Negro population.

About the time that these unfavorable economic conditions in the southern districts were most powerful, there came an unusual demand for labor in northern industrial centers. Prior to this, these industrial districts had been

The causes and effects of general Negro migration have been discussed in an article by the writer in The Annals of the American Academy of Political and Social Science, Vol. XLIX, Sept., 1913; also in his monograph, The Negro at Work in New York City, Columbia University Studies in History, Economics and Public Law, Vol. XLIX. No. 3 pp. 13-44.

largely supplied by semi-skilled emigrant workers from Europe. The Great War stopped this labor supply. At the same time the overwhelming demand of War orders created an unprecedented need of labor in northern centers. Northern employers in casting about for workers soon discovered the unworked Negro labor supply of the South.

The offer of two, three, four and five dollars a day in northern industrial centers was an irresistible influence to Negro workmen who were getting one dollar, one dollar and a half and two dollars a day in southern communities. The relative increase in the cost of food, shelter, clothing and other necessities of life did not count in the wage-earner's mind. For he was thinking in terms of money wages not real wages. Many do not consider that higher wages and higher cost of living usually go together.

Social Causes of Migration

Although economic causes are important we should not overlook the fact that other influences have borne these people northward. This has been true not only for the past twelve months but probably for the past forty years. Poor housing and neighborhood conditions, poor schools for their children, "Jim crow" cars, disfranchisement, lack of justice in courts, mob violence and many of the other unfavorable conditions of every-day life, have created a feeling of unrest among southern Negroes. Because of such conditions and in spite of the fact that wages are good in some localities, Negroes have left in large numbers for northern communities, believing that there they would find greater freedom and better treatment.

Like down-trodden people the world over, these masses are struggling to get away from the hard and restricted conditions of certain southern localities and are seeking the advantages and the liberty of better communities. People will endure being poorly paid, half fed, poorly clad; living in poor houses; having poor schools for their children; being limited in many of the other opportunities of life when they believe they can do no better. But when they believe they see opportunities to get better wages, better food, better clothes, better houses, better schools for their children, and greater freedom, they may be mistaken in what they think they will get, they may blunder in trying to get it, but they know what they want and will seek it.

7

The extent and causes of this general migration concern us here only to the extent that Detroit has been one of the principal northern cities to which the new-comers have come in large numbers.

2.—NEW-COMERS TO DETROIT, MICHIGAN.

During this migration of the past two years Detroit, the leading center of the automobile industry has been one of the principal points of destination for these migrants, mainly from Alabama, Georgia, Florida, and Tennessee.

The Population and Its Location

Within the past five years it is estimated that the Negro population of this city has increased more than fourfold. In 1910 the United States Census recorded 5741 Negro inhabitants of Detroit. Conservative estimates now place the number between 25,000 and 35,000. Probably more than three-fourths of this increase has taken place during the past two years. Of course, Detroit as a whole has greatly increased in population. In 1910, its census return showed a total population of 465,766. The present total population is conservatively estimated to be from 750,000 to 800,000.

Naturally the settlement of these Negro new-comers in this city has created far-reaching community problems. The problem of housing, for instance, has been greatly intensified because of the rapid increase of other elements of the city's population. For many years preceding 1915, Detroit had a small Negro population. It consisted mainly of families of a high grade both in intelligence and well-being. They lived in various parts of the city, self-respecting and respected for their intelligence and moral character. Some of them held responsible places in the business, professional and community life of the city.

About ten years ago, the crusade in other sections of the Country against race-tracks and the popularity of a race-track at Windsor, Canada, just across the river from Detroit, brought many Negroes of the undesirable type to the city. The freedom from police intereference caused Detroit to be known as a "wide-open town." Disreputable characters of other kinds than those who follow the race-track were drawn from other large cities. The beginning of a Negro ghetto in the region of St. Antoine and Hastings Streets and Adams Avenue was made.

Then came the Great War. The industrial demands of Detroit for laborers became imperative. Negroes were drawn to the city by the hundreds daily. These newcomers were usually of the honest, industrious type who were seeking conditions better than those under which they were living. They were for the most part unskilled and with little education but were seeking better things.

These people have had to find their homes largely in the crowded Negro district which had been formed before their influx. As the population grew it expanded North to about Rowena Street and South to about Macomb, within about 20 city blocks—some of the blocks are small compared with the size of a usual city block. They were overcrowded in this district. They overflowed toward the North beyond Brady Street, toward the South below Lafayette Street, toward the East beyond Rivard Street and toward the West to about Beaubien Street. They share the neighborhood with kindly Jews. Toward the North end of the district Jews predominate. Going toward the East they have pushed into an Italian neighborhood.

Negroes have found residence in smaller numbers in other neighborhoods than this main district. In these, they are not so decidedly segregated as in the larger area. In the Western part of the city they have located in four neighborhoods in sufficient numbers to be clearly noticeable. The first locality is bounded by Warren Avenue (West) on the north, the Grand Trunk Railroad on the South, 23rd Street on the East and McKinley Avenue on the West. The second West side neighborhood where Negroes have found homes is bounded by Moore Place, Warren Avenue, Grand Boulevard West, and Woodrow Avenue. The third West side neighborhood where Negroes have found shelter is bounded by McGraw Avenue, Kirby Avenue, 14th Avenue, and Stanton Avenue.

On the Eastern side of the city they have found houses in the neighborhood bounded by Holbrook Avenue on the North, Melbourne Avenue on the South, St. Aubin Avenue on the East and Brush Street on the West. There is a considerable settlement in Hamtramck, which is a suburb "so continuous with the city of Detroit that the division line of political authority is artificial." Also, here and there in both the Eastern and Western sections of the city proper, a few Negro families have been able to secure houses in several different localities.

Segregation of Negro New-Comers

There has been a tendency toward the neighborhood segregation of the new-comers. Partly as a result of this, a sharp division has developed between the new-comers and the old residents. During the earlier days in Detroit the old residents, as pointed out above, enjoyed a large share in the general life and activity of the community. With the large increase in the number of Negroes and the coming of many of the less desirable type, there was a reaction of these older residents against a gradual tending toward the segregation of all Negroes. There was also a class feeling growing out of their more favorable conditions.

Length of Residence

The large majority of this population has come to the city within the last eighteen months. Besides the testimony of observers to this effect, we have the reports on the length of time that 407 heads of families had been residing in Detroit. The figures show that of 286 heads of families whose length of residence was ascertained, 212 had been in Detroit less than 18 months. The details as to length of residence of these heads of families were as follows: 33 men and 3 women had been in the city less than 6 months; 102 men and 9 women had been there 6 months to 11 months; 61 men and 4 women, 11 months to 17 months.; 4 men and 1 woman, 18 months to 23 months. There were 62 men and 7 women who had been in the city 2 years or more. The length of residence of 121 was doubtful or unknown.

In many instances in addition to making the adjustment from the rural districts to urban centers these Negroes have had to adjust themselves to life in a northern center differing from the South in climate, type of industry and community life. The concrete necessities of employment, housing, health, recreation and the conservation of the family life including children have been a part of the inevitable demands made upon them.

The Problems of the Christian Church

Confronting this situation these strangers in a strange land have needed not alms but friends to assist them. The question for our consideration and solution then is, how may the Christian church thru its members and organization so extend its service to these people as to help them make the necessary adjustments not only in such concrete needs as employment, housing, recreation, health, but also in obtaining a firm hold upon those ethical and religious ideals which will make them an asset and not a liability to the community into which they have come?

The solution we seek involves the answer to such questions as these: What is the industrial opportunity of these Negroes? What is the impression of employers as to their reliability and efficiency as workmen? Will a large number of them become permanent residents? What are the present housing conditions they have and in what ways may these conditions be improved? What provision has been made for recreation and amusement during their leisure? What is the present status of their churches as actual and potential agencies for moral and religious motive power? What social agencies are available for helping their community life? How can the church of the several denominations co-operate with the social agencies and thus help to meet the industrial needs? How can these churches co-operate with the social agencies in helping to meet the needs for better housing? How can they in the same way help to meet requirements for recreation and for family life? What are the church and religious needs and how can the denominations help to meet them? There were neither time nor available data to treat of the questions of health, of children and education, of crime and several other community questions affecting the religion of the church in respect to these new-comers.

The Aim of this Cursory Survey.

To find the facts and analyze their meaning so as to assist partially in answering some of these questions; to formulate a practical program of action for the churches co-operating among themselves, and to propose a plan for the co-operation of the churches with the social agencies and the co-operation of white and colored people, have been the aim of such a cursory survey of the situation as the time at the disposal of the investigator had allowed.

No claim is set up that the indications here are final, nor that the program does not need modification or revision. Both modification and revision will doubtless be needed as additional study of the community is made and as parts of the proposed program are adapted to meet the situation.

11

CHAPTER II.

The Industrial Opportunity.

For decades the Negro enjoyed civic privileges in the North but suffered from industrial disfranchisement. He was confined to some of the domestic and personal service occupations. He was probably losing ground in these until the industrial demand of the Great War came.

Negro Workers Now in Demand

The pressing need of the Detroit enterprises for laborers caused her industrial captains to make unprecedented wage advances. This drew thousands of workmen from all parts of the country. Her enterprises were also opened now to the Negro workmen in greater numbers than were dreamed of before this time. The question ceased to be whether or not Negroes could find jobs but rather what kind of jobs were they fitted for. The problem now is not one of Negroes finding work but of doing the work open to them with such efficiency and satisfaction that when the pressing need of the War inflated industry is past their labor will be wanted along with that of other labor groups.

The available evidence that Detroit has removed the barriers from the employment of Negroes in many lines is considerable. Between July 2 and December 23, employers made calls for 5542 male and 317 female Negro workers, thru bonafide requests that came to the employment office run by the Detroit Urban League in co-operation with the Employers Association of Detroit. The large majority of the men were wanted by the automobile factories, the principal industry of the city. These firms demanded mainly unskilled men. About 29.3 per cent of these calls specified unskilled laborers and about 43.9 were miscellaneous calls for men unspecified, mainly unskilled laborers. A large proportion of the calls were for men to work as domestic and personal servants.

A Proportion of Skilled and Semi-skilled Workers

But it is significant that there were calls for 336 truckers (automobile), 160 moulders, 109 machinists (unspecified), 45 core-makers and for a number of other miscellaneous skilled and semi-skilled men. Most of the women were wanted in domestic and personal service in private homes.

But it should be noted that 32 calls came from a garment factory, 18 from a cigar factory and 19 for ushers in a theatre.

Table 1, which follows shows in detail the kind of work for which these laborers were wanted, with the number of laborers of each kind requested:

Table 1.—Showing Number of Male and Female Workers Requested by Employers thru the Joint Employment Office and the Detroit Urban League July 2 to December 23, 1917.

Male

Laborers	846	Metal Carriers	16
Laborers (outside)	778	Tool makers	15
Truckers (automobile)	336	Repair-Vacuum Cleaners	14
Janitors	225	Riveters	8
Moulders	160	Metal (unspecified)	7
Machinists (unspecified)	109	Cutters (unspecified)	6
Porters (unspecified)	102	Watchmen	6
Laborers' Helpers	69	Assembly men (automobile)	5
Yardmen	67	Assembly Men Helpers	26
Kitchen men and Dishwashers	54	Farm (unspecified)	3
Furnace Tenders	70	Block testers	2
Mechanics	48	Pipe Layers	2
Core-makers	45	Rivet Buckers	2
Housemen and bell-boys	28	Paper-hangers	2
Chauffeurs and Crankmen	10	Miscellaneous (mainly unspecified)	2431
Elevator men	26		
Coal passers (laborers)	24	Total	5542

Female

Laundry (day)	123	Factory (cigar)	18
Maids	45	Cook	15
Factory (Garment)	32	Office	2
Dishwashers	24	Miscellaneous	14
General Housework	25		
Ushers (Theatre)	19	Total	317

Are Negroes Meeting the Calls?   Yes.

A natural question follows: Are the Negroes meeting these calls? The Negroes in large numbers are filling the places offered them. This may be seen in the statement of the Urban League's employment office that, with the year ending November 15, 1917, it had placed about 10,000 Negro workers, men and women. In checking over the detailed monthly records of this office, it appeared that roughly estimated about four-fifths of those placed consisted of men and about one-fifth consisted of women.

Distribution in Occupations

The table below contains the reported number of Negroes employed by some of the large firms at the end of April, 1917. They consist mainly of the Negroes employed by automobile firms or firms making automobile parts or accessories. The Burroughs Adding Machine Company, the Studebaker Corporation, the Cadillac Motor Car Company, the Maxwell Motor Car Company, the Dodge Brothers Motor Car Company, the Timken Detroit Axle Works and the Detroit Brass Works were employing Negroes but the numbers were not given. Table II. gives the firms and the number of Negroes they were employing on April 27, 1917:

Table II.—Showing Number of Negro Workmen Employed on April 27, 1917, by Firms with which Detroit Urban League had touch.

Packard Motor Car Co. (May 18)	1100
Buhl Malleable Iron Co.	280
Ford Motor Car Co.	200
Continental Motor Car Co.	200
Aluminum Castings Co.	150
Michigan Steel Castings	170
Michigan Copper and Brass	125
Michigan Central Railroad	100
Michigan Malleable Iron Co.	100
General Aluminum and Brass	65
Chalmers Motor Car Co.	62
Detroit Pressed Steel	50
Hudson Motor Car Co.	50
Detroit Stove Works	27
Paige Detroit Motor Car Co	20
Saxon Motor Car Co.	20
Hupp Motor Car Co.	20
Detroit Seamless Tubes Co.	20
Monarch Foundry	15
Michigan Smelting & Refining	100
Estimated Total	2874

In the report from which the preceding figures were taken there is the following statement: "There are many other firms that we have been unable to reach employing Negro laborers in large numbers. There is a number of smaller factories and foundries employing Negroes in numbers under fifteen, the majority of whom we have not listed here. The majority of the firms above are anxious to employ many more Negroes than are represented by the figures."

The distribution of Negroes in the various occupations may also be seen in the occupations of 407 heads of families interviewed in a house-to-house canvass made by an investigator for the Board of Health. Of the 362 men who were heads of families, 122 were laborers, 35 were mechanics (unskilled), 11 were porters (unskilled), 5 were automobile and truck drivers, 7 were hostlers, 8 were moulders, 8 machinists. There were 6 barbers, 12 janitors, 1 chauffeur, 3 waiters, 2 cooks, 1 contractor, 1 painter, 3 plasterers, 3 motormen, 1 cooper, 2 carpenters, 3 watchmen, 3 cement finishers, 10 teamsters, 3 garbage, 2 lawyers, 3 ministers, 1 musician, 3 privates in U. S. Army, 19 miscellaneous, 5 unemployed, 79 unknown.

Of the 45 women, there were 12 doing day's work, 10 housekeepers taking roomers, 6 laundresses, 2 hairdressers, 1 nurse (unspecified), 1 seamstress, 1 cook, 1 woman receiving a pension (unspecified), 4 miscellaneous (unspecified) and 7 unknown.

The three sets of figures given above—the number of requests for Negro workers, the number of Negroes employed by local firms and the occupations of the heads of 407 families—are very instructive in showing the great industrial opportunity of the Negro in Detroit. The demand is very large and has been rather constant for a number of months. The occupations cover a wide range and the greater number of occupations are outside of domestic and personal service.

Negroes with Skill Will Increase

As is to be expected for the present and for some time to come, practically all of these workers are unskilled or semi-skilled. Although realizing how dangerous it is to forecast, one may yet reasonably predict that some of these Negroes will gradually work their way into the skilled departments of the industries. The demands for skill, intelligence and aptitude of the better grade of workers will

15

gradually cause many more to be introduced into skilled processes.

Detroit is an "open shop town." The Negroes, therefore, who show skill or capacity to develop it will not be barred in most cases because union workmen combine against them. Here and there in small numbers or in small shops they will probably be given jobs requiring skill. Gradually a body of mechanics efficient and skilled in different lines will develop. Employers will be able to secure sufficient numbers to ignore threats against the employment of Negro workmen, if such should be made.

The industrial opportunity is partly determined by the wages workmen receive. The only available figures on wages were those of the heads of 407 families interviewed in the house-to-house canvass, previously mentioned. The wages of the other men were reported by the month. Their monthly wages were as follows: 1 received between $30 and $39, 3 received between $40 and $49 per month, 6 received between $60 and $69; 29 received between $70 and $79; 96 received between $80 and $89; 6 received between $90 and $99; 27 received between $100 and $119; 21 received between $120 and $129, and 4 received $140 or more per month. There was 1 man working at $6.30 per day. The number of days he was employed per month could not be ascertained. There were 161 men whose monthly wages were doubtful or unknown; 2 men were the owners of a business and 5 were unemployed.

The wages of the 45 women who were heads of families were as follows: 13 women were doing day's work at $2 per day and 1 at $2.50 per day, but the number of days they were employed could not be ascertained and so the monthly wages could not be calculated. There were 2 women earning between $40 and $49 per month and 3 earning between $70 and $79 per month. The monthly wages of 26 were doubtful or unknown.

Prevailing Wages.

As far as these figures are typical of the wages of Negro workmen in Detroit, they show that the prevailing wages of the men are from about $70 to about $119 per month. For 159 of the 194 men whose wages were ascertained were receiving wages ranging between these amounts. The prevailing wage for women is about that of those doing day work, $2 per day. It is common knowledge that there

16

are very few places in the South where a house-to-house canvass of Negro families would show such a high range of wages.

Cost of Living.

Of course, money wages should be considered in the light of the cost of living. Satisfactory figures on cost of food and clothing could not be gathered in the time available. The U. S. Bureau of Labor statistics on retail prices in Southern cities and in Detroit are hardly applicable as there were no figures later than 1915. Rent costs in Detroit are decidedly higher than in the South as is shown by Chapter III. on housing. Several families of intelligent new-comers, were questioned about their experience in regard to the relative cost of food and clothing in Detroit and in the Southern cities from which they had come. They said taking the same quality into account there is not a considerable difference. This, of course, would not hold good for the new-comers from Southern rural districts who did not have to buy some of their necessities. It also does not take into account the greater amount and better quality of clothing required in a Northern climate.

The next and last question is how permanently will the Negro establish himself in the Detroit labor market? Employers are reported as having different views about the suitability of Negro labor for their needs. But the fact stands out clearly that practically every large firm recorded as having Negro laborers has continued to employ them. Most of these firms have considerably increased the number they employed at the beginning.

Opinions of Employers

The opinion expressed by several able observers may be summed up in the gist of an interesting statement given by Mr. Chas. M. Culver, General Manager of the Detroit Employers Association. This association includes in its membership the leading firms and employers of the city. He thought some employers were highly pleased with Negro workmen and some were not. He said, "There are two lines of adverse opinion about the Negro as a workman: First, nine-tenths of the complaints of employers against the Negro is that he is too slow. He does not make the speed that the routine of efficient industry demands.

He is lacking in the regularity demanded by the routine of industry day by day.

"Second, the Negro has been observed to be disinclined to work out-of-doors when the cold weather comes. Employers have discussed this and have not found the Negro satisfactory on this point. Unless the Negroes overcome this practice employers will turn to other sources of supply when their present extreme needs are past. Employers must have a labor supply upon which they can depend at all seasons, laborers who will work out-of-doors winter as well as summer."

Negro Women in Industry

Another important fact bearing upon the matter of permanence of the Negro's industrial opportunity in Detroit relates to colored women as workers. The A. Krolik Company, large garment manufacturers, have successfully carried thru an experiment that is being watched with interest by other firms in Detroit and elsewhere. They have opened and, so far, successfully operated a pants factory, using colored women entirely in doing the work, including the office work, except the management. The investigator talked with Mr. Cohen, the superintendent who has carried thru the project, also with one of the members of the Krolik family who has been personally interested in the enterprise on humanitarian grounds in addition to the business interest.

They both testified that the experiment is now assuredly upon a successful footing. Mr. Cohen said his greatest difficulty was in overcoming the timidity of the girls and inducing them to believe they can make successful operatives and earn good wages. The factory conditions under which the work is done are very good. Also, one of the largest theatres has begun to employ colored girls as ushers. They are proving satisfactory.

Instruction Needed for Women Who Work as Domestic Servants

On the other hand, large numbers of the women who have come to Detroit during the migration have capacity only for the simplest kind of domestic service. Many of them who must work are so untrained that they are unemployable even in laundering, cleaning and other domestic service in private homes. This fact makes a serious situation.

During the time of the writer's visit to Detroit there was a movement started in the city by the Detroit Urban League to provide some instruction for this class of women which would enable them to be placed in day's work and similar domestic service.

We may now summarize the indications of the Negro's industrial opportunity: The calls from firms showed a large demand for Negro men. About two-thirds of the calls were for unskilled laborers, the very type of workmen Negroes are easily able to supply. Probably between 10 and 12 per cent of the calls were for semi-skilled and skilled workers. Large numbers of Negroes are employed by firms making automobiles or automobile accessories. Reports from 20 of the largest firms last April showed 2874 then employed by them. The majority of these firms were ready to employ many more Negroes and many smaller firms were using them. The success of the A. Krolik Company in starting Negro women to work in the garment trades may open another great source of income for this Negro group.

Summary

There is undoubtedly a large industrial opportunity for Negroes in Detroit. Since many employers who are already employing Negroes are pleased and are seeking more of them and since the Krolik experiment with women workers is proving a success, we may reasonably expect the Negro worker to gain a permanent hold in the Detroit industries. This means that most of the Negroes who have come to the city will remain and that others will follow.

What can the churches do to help the new-comers make this great industrial opportunity permanent? Some of the industrial needs of these new-comers which the churches could help supply stand out clearly.

What Churches Can Do

First and foremost, they need some provision for training in the processes of the occupations in which so many of them are now entering. This can be done by three means: First, part time arrangements might be made with firms where they are employed for some system of vocational education correlated with the work they are doing. Second, night schools offering an education in skilled and semi-skilled occupations as well as in the English branches might be opened. The community should be led to supply this thru its public school system. Third, special afternoon and evening courses in domestic science for women and girls who must earn their living in domestic and personal service.

On the first item, the churches with the co-operation of the Detroit Urban League might work quietly thru intelligent laymen to lay this matter before foremen, superintendents and owners of factories where these laymen are employed. Thus they could create a sentiment in favor of such a plan. On the second item, the leading members of the churches may unite with the League in securing such provision as mentioned above from the public school officials and if necessary in seeing that public funds were provided. On the third item, the churches could furnish money to start special courses of instruction in domestic science for women and girls.

A second need is stimulation to overcome the industrial ideas and habits brought from the South. The Negro workmen's slowness and irregularity mentioned by those whose opinions were sought are largely due to industrial habits brought from a Southern environment.

The churches could provide lectures, social study classes and intelligent workers for the personal touch in workshop and home to help overcome these faults. A system of friendly home visitation might be organized. A considerable part of the complaint about Negro workers "quitting" when cold weather comes can be removed by instruction in how to dress and in simple repeated assurances that they need not fear freezing to death if they are properly clad. The churches can give larger support to the "Dress Well Club" which has been already organized. Lectures on food and dress could be supplied by the churches.

Again, every individual Negro needs to have it brought home to him by constant reminder that all the Negro workmen are on trial in the face of unusual industrial opportunities and that individually they must make good for the sake of all their fellow workmen. This is largely the work of preachment from the pulpit and the platform. What a world of service is open here to the Negro churches!

CHAPTER III.

Housing and Recreation.

1.—Housing.

Housing a Pressing Problem

Perhaps the most pressing problem the new-comers have had to meet is that of housing. Houses for families involve not only the question of physical shelter but the problem of sanitary and moral environment.

Where rent is so high that lodgers must be taken in to help pay it, the strain upon family life is serious. When the demand for houses is great, there is little choice as to neighborhood, and little power of protection against the neglect of sanitary provision and exploitation by landlords. The Negro new-comers to Detroit the past two years have faced all these conditions. At the present time, probably 12,000 to 15,000 Negro residents are squeezed into the largest district bounded by Brady, Lafayette, Rivard and Baubien Streets, described in the introduction. This is a district which formerly furnished housing accommodations for less than one-half that number.

"Buffet Flats"

One observer said he had "seen rooms occupied by two people where the most convenient way to dress was to stand in the middle of the bed." While this is probably a witty exaggeration, it is true that many of the buildings are very badly overcrowded and are nothing more than dilapidated shacks. The investigation of the Urban League showed that the usual size of houses or apartments is 3, 4 or 5 rooms. Many of them are in the midst of saloons, gambling places or "buffet flats." The "buffet flat" is a sort of high-class combination of a gambling parlor, a "blind tiger" and an apartment of prostitution. It is especially dangerous because it is usually in a private house in a neighborhood of homes, is run with all signs of respectability and caters especially to the youthful and unwary.

21

Size of Houses and Apartments.

The size of houses and apartments and rents paid for them may be judged from the records of 407 families visited by the Board of Health investigator. The number of rooms in houses or apartments occupied by these 407 families was as follows: There were 63 families each living in one room, 24 families each living in 2 rooms, 34 families each living in 3 rooms, 35 families each living in 4 rooms, 71 families each living in 5 rooms, 44 families each living in 6 rooms, 43 families were each living in 7 rooms, 13 in 8 rooms each, 14 in 9 rooms each, and 16 families were each living in 10 to 12 rooms. There were 50 families about which such information was not available.

The Lodger Evil.

It should be emphasized that many of the families living in from 1 to 4 rooms were accommodating lodgers and that practically all the families recorded as living in 5 or more rooms were taking lodgers to help pay the rent, and that all the families except 6 that were living in 7 or more rooms had 2 or more lodgers. In fact, many of the homes of this size were run either as rooming houses for profit or because the necessity of paying the high rents had made them practically so.

Rents Paid.

That we may see clearly that the rents were high let us look at the amounts paid for these houses and apartments. The first figures are those of rents paid by the 407 families the size of whose houses or apartments have just been described. The monthly rent paid by heads of families by groups is as follows: There were 3 who were paying below $10 per month; 27 were paying between $10 and $11 per month; all these were living in one room apartments. There were 57 heads of families who were paying monthly rent between $15 and $19; the large majority of these were 1 and 2 room apartments. There were 43 heads of families who were paying $20 to $24 monthly rent; 39 were paying $25 to $29; 29 were paying between $30 and $34; 45 were paying between $35 and $39; 21 were paying between $40 and $44; 13 were paying between $45 and $54, and 4 were paying $60 and above. Some of those paying the higher rent were subletting. There were 31 heads of families who were owners or were buying and 94 whose rent payments were unknown. Some of these rents seem reasonable, but when considered in the light of the poor houses for which they are paid, they are not.

These figures show that the prevailing rents paid by these families are from $20 per month to $44 per month, because 177 of 282 heads of families whose rents were known were paying rents within the limits of these amounts.

Size of Families.

If we view these figures relating to the sizes of house or apartment, to lodgers, and to rents in connection with the figures for size of the 407 families, we get an idea of considerable over-crowding. Excluding lodgers, there were **18** families consisting of 1 person; 169 families of 2 persons; 108 families of 3; 51 families of 4; 28 families of 5; 19 families of 6; 10 families of 7; 3 families of 8 and 1 family of 9 persons. This made a total of 1,241 individuals. There were 217 families, more than 50 per cent of the 407 families, which consisted of 2 or 3 persons. If we add the families consisting of 4 persons we have 268 families. The prevailing size of a family among these 407 families was from 2 to 4 persons, exclusive of lodgers. If we add the facts about lodgers we have before us the picture of the pressing problem. There were 7 families living in 1 room and keeping lodgers; 146 families were living in 2 or more rooms and keeping lodgers; only 100 families were reported as having no lodgers and 98 were doubtful or unknown. Here we have a pressure against wholesome family life which is serious in the extreme.

Size of Families.

With reference to over-crowding and rents, Mr. Washington of the Urban League said last May: "The houses inhabited by the colored people in this district vary, but on the whole they are the least desirable in the city. Houses of 4 or 5 rooms crowded with people pay the highest possible rents. Of 100 houses, about 50 consisted of 4 or 5 rooms, with no bath, and frequently no inside toilet. And in no case was less than $20 per month rent charged. In most instances, $30 to $35 was the rent per month for 5 rooms. The average rent per room was $5.90."

The same investigation showed that this is higher rent than the average figures given by the Visiting House-keepers' Association for the whole city, which is $4.25 per room. The statement was made that during the past eighteen months rents for houses occupied by colored people had increased from 50 per cent to 350 per cent.

The conveniences in the larger number of these houses may be judged by whether or not they have bathrooms. Of the 407 homes visited in the house-to-house canvass, 195 only were known to have bathrooms; 118 were definitely known not to have any, and 94 were doubtful or unknown. In a section of the country where a house with a bathroom is the rule, these people have paid exorbitant prices for small houses without this necessary convenience.

That the conditions described above are typical for houses occupied by Negroes is beyond question.

2.—Recreation.

What workers do when they are employed is largely governed by the dictates of their employers. What they do in their leisure is largely determined by their own de-sires. These desires are largely the result of the recrea-tional opportunities and forces which influence the workers. The way leisure is used in recreation and amusement in turn profoundly affects the efficiency of the workers in their industrial activity. Their recreation and amusement have no less an influence on their personal morals and com-munity life.

Theatres.

The question, then, of the recreation and amusement of these Negro new-comers is a most important matter. The survey of provision for play for the children and library facilities for all was not included because of a lack of time. There is a moving picture theatre near the largest Negro neighborhood. This is largely patronized by Negroes. Another "movie" house near the same neighborhood has recently been turned to vaudeville performances in Hebrew, and so no longer is an attraction for Negroes. A third thea-tre, a playhouse owned by a colored proprietor and using colored talent, has a reputation for fairly clean shows, although there is considerable testimony about question-able shows and "stunts" presented.

Pool-room and Dance-halls.

The other principal indoor amusement for the men is at the pool-rooms. The pool-rooms do an active business. They vary with the type of men to whom they cater. Those visited during Christmas week were all crowded. Gambling was reported in connection with some of them. There are frequent dances for men and women. The admission fees to the dances are rather high, usually fifty cents per person.

To secure wholesome amusement and recreation the following movements in this direction have been fostered by the Detroit Urban League. To offset the high admission fees to the dances and also to furnish wholesome surroundings, that is, dances where no liquor is sold and good order is preserved, the Young Negroes' Progressive Club is promoting what is known as a "community dance." This dance is held in one of the public buildings. The admission is ten cents per person. The surplus proceeds of the dance are used for promoting other community activities. Attendance of new-comers is especially sought. This dance closes at 11:00 p. m., in contrast with others that run until 2:00 a. m., 3:00 a. m. or even 4:00 a. m.

For athletic sports, last summer a baseball league was a star feature of the community and weekly drew crowds out to one of the baseball parks. Last fall a football team was similarly promoted. During the winter basket-ball has been started successfully in the gymnasium of the Cass High School, under the auspices of the City Recreation Commission.

For the girls, a Camp Fire under a colored guardian has been developed, and for the boys the Boy Scout organization has enlisted a company of colored scouts.

This is about the sum of recreation and amusement open to this large number of Negro new-comers. They are here in a more liberal atmosphere than they have known before. Many of them have shorter hours of work than before coming to the city. The use of their leisure in wholesome recreation and amusement is of paramount importance for their welfare as well as for that of the community at large. Here is a great field for church co-operation with the League that has started these efforts, a field needing inspiration and leadership the Church alone can give.

Summary and Suggestions on Housing and Recreation.

Let us sum up the few facts on housing and recreation and add some recommendations which naturally follow.

The majority of the houses are in very bad repair, many of them actual shanties. Less than one-half of the houses probably have bath-rooms or inside toilets. The rents are exceedingly high. The average rent per room of these houses occupied by Negroes has been estimated at $5.90, while the estimated average rent per room for the city at large is $4.25. The prevailing rent per family ranges between $20 per month and $44 per month. These rents on houses occupied by colored people have had an estimated increase during the past eighteen months from 50 per cent to as much as 350 per cent in some cases.

Excluding the heads of families, from whom information in regard to lodgers was not secured, of 309 heads of families, there were 209 which kept lodgers. Taken in connection with the number of rooms occupied per family, the figures indicate overcrowding and other strains upon family life that are very serious. The conveniences and the privacy of the house largely determine the health and integrity of the home.

What can be done to remedy these conditions? The leaders of the Detroit Urban League have carefully studied the local housing situation and any effort to help the situation might be co-ordinated with theirs.

They propose that certain factories employing Negroes be induced to build houses for their workmen on land which the factories already own near their plants. Further, it has been pointed out that in the Negro district there are many one-story and one-and-a-half story houses which could easily be remodeled to accommodate two or more families in small, comfortable apartments.

In addition to the League's proposal, the matter of city regulation of overcrowding and city requirements for conveniences such as toilets and water supply for all tenanted houses may be studied, including photographic exhibits. This information might be used and remedies sought through the city government. It may mean a longer time in getting relief, but it may be made a benefit to larger numbers than any other plan. Of course, such an effort for the Negroes should be made a part of a general program for the whole city if possible. The churches could be of great help in this connection.

The white churches also could help with the building of model apartment houses through the interest of wealthy laymen who look with favor upon "5 per cent philanthropy."

The recreation movements in baseball, football and basketball are excellent. The "community dance" idea can be spread

26

to include more people and a large number of evenings by opening several different school buildings in several neighborhoods. The small provision for wholesome amusement in theatres and moving pictures can wisely be increased by organized sentiment for patronage to enterprising managers and proprietors who undertake to furnish such amusement. The large number of heavily attended pool-rooms call for some plan of organized supervision. A campaign for law enforcement should close up the "buffet flats." Is not this a work for the churches, white and colored?

CHAPTER IV.

The Church and the People.

Their Churches Their Principal Organization.

The highest expression of both individual and group life of Negroes is through their churches. Their churches are an expression of their instincts and desires for a "prosperity policy." As has been suggested in the preceding pages, the Negro new-comers can be very effectively influenced through this medium to meet their employment, housing, recreation, health and other social needs. Through the churches also the ideals of the Christ may be presented and embraced as a preparation for action in the home, the school, the workshop and the street. What, then, is the present equipment, location and leadership of the churches?

In trying to form an approximate idea of the present church forces among Negroes in Detroit the investigator attempted to get data on the churches and the ministers. That which is presented here can be counted only approximately accurate, for more time for the study was needed. The reported facts could be checked up in only a few cases. Some of the items on the value of church property are probably wide of the mark. Indebtedness, money raised for all purposes, that spent for improvements and in payment of church debts during the preceding year are approximately correct. The membership reported for the churches, Sunday Schools and young people's societies represents reported enrollment. It is safe to say that the active membership and regular attendance are probably considerably less.

There are five colored Protestant Churches, which have a considerable membership and good buildings. The ministers of these are men of education, strong personality, high moral character and of great influence both with their people and in the community. The Catholic Church, St. Peter Claver, has an excellent structure. Upon a visit to the church, the priest was away, and a second visit could not be made.

The other nine churches are small and each has a reported membership, with one exception, of less than 200. This probably means an active working membership of probably a fourth less. Their ministers are men of limited education and training. Some of them, of course, are poorly fitted for their profession.

Principal Denominations Represented.

It is highly important to note, however, the number of denominations represented. There are Baptist, Protestant, Episcopal, A. M. E., A. M. E. Zion, C. M. E., M. E. and Catholic churches. It is significant, too, that the Baptist and Methodist denominations have the largest number of churches. These are the two denominations which have the largest number of Negro communicants in the country. Another factor of far-reaching importance is that these churches have been very largely started and almost entirely supported by the Negroes themselves. They have the impulse to go ahead and do. They need guidance and instruction in how to do.

Location of Churches.

Of the fifteen churches of which the locations are secured, thirteen were in or adjacent to the main Negro district, that is, between Superior Street on the North, Mullet Street on the South, Dubois Street on the East and Beaubien Street on the West. There is one small church on the West side of the city and one in Hamtramck. Five of the 13 churches in or near the principal Negro district are within a few blocks of each other and six others are in two groups not so far apart.

Other Significant Points.

The reports from ten of these churches bring out some other points of significance. With the exception of one church, the proportion of members in the Sunday School and the young people's societies is comparatively small. This probably indicates that the young people are not offered avenues of action which would hold them by satisfying their natural desire to do something.

The apparent good financial condition of the Negro churches for which reports were secured shows that there are money resources available for whatever these churches have undertaken. Only three churches, two of them organized in 1917, reported debts on their church buildings and grounds and one of these was for less than $5,000. Eight of the ten churches reported ownership of parsonage and other property; some of this property carried mortgages. Seven reported from $2,000 to $12,000 raised for all purposes during the preceding twelve months. In view of the usual financial condition of Negro churches, this is a good showing. It offers, too, good ground for high hopes of larger service to the community when these potential resources are coupled with larger undertakings.

Churches and Industrial Efficiency.

One of the very important questions that involve the church is its present relation to and influence in improving the industrial, housing and recreation conditions of the Negro population. The influence of the church in the industrial activity of Negroes is shown in a statement of Mr. Forrester B. Washington, director of the Detroit Urban League. He said: "We have placed over 10,000 Negroes in work during the past twelve months. They have come from all sources, club-rooms, pool-rooms, railway stations and churches. We have found that one class of Negroes are invariably making good. That class is those referred by the churches. I mean this not from an ecclesiastical or denominational standpoint, but from a standpoint of business. I wish all of the 10,000 who have been placed by us could have been secured through the churches because, from our experience, I believe they would have been diligent, regular and zealous in their work." This fact may be explained in two ways. First, the type of Negro workman who is attracted to the church is likely to be the type that is sober, industrious and reliable. Second, church attendance helps to make most workmen into such a type. There is probably truth in both interpretations. They both emphasize in a superlative degree the industrial value of the church to the new-comers and to the community which benefits by their labor. It gives additional evidence, too, of the social power and value of the church. The colored churches have also been the best avenues of advertising for Negro workers.

Principal Church Need Is Efficiency in Existing Churches.

In summarizing this chapter, we can say that the facts of the preceding paragraph show that the problem here is not so much the establishment of new churches as it is helping the churches already established to do efficiently the great work which is possible for them to do. As the population grows, doubtless more churches will be needed. The main need, however, now is to make the existing churches stronger and more efficient for the work of religious and social betterment. The people have an inherited attachment for their churches. The churches therefore should be helped to meet both the religious and community needs of the people. Instead of being forced to work for the community through the pressure of outside agencies, let the churches inspire and instruct its members, and lead them forth to direct the forces of the growing community life. So far as could be ascertained, the churches, white and colored, have done little direct work in improving housing conditions. Some of the ministers have spoken of such needs in public; church members have discussed it in private. But the challenge of the situation to the churches has not been met either with plans or money for changing the conditions.

Relation of Churches to Recreation.

The churches are also challenged to meet the demands of the use of leisure. They have already taken some part in the work. One of the churches undertook to equip a gymnasium, but finally saw that a community effort of the same kind in one of the public schools if given support would reach larger numbers. The minister said publicly that he would join in the community effort. The fact is that the present lack of community betterment activity of the denominations the Country over is leaving the every-day life needs of the Negroes to be met by activities which draw a large part of their support from other sources than the churches. But the masses of the Negroes are largely influenced by their religious attachment to their churches. If the churches, white and colored, do not meet the challenge of these every-day needs two results must inevitably follow: First, the more intelligent type of Negroes will lose some interest in the church because it ceases to help them in their most pressing problems of every-day life. Second, the less intelligent type will probably be led into forms of religious fervor toward religious results that do not connect with the active ethics and pressing problems of the day.

What the churches of Detroit may do is to unite the fervor of evangelism with the practical power of mighty works that reach the concrete community needs. Here is the opportunity for the white and colored churches to demonstrate the power of religion as a solvent of the most difficult social and racial problems.

Informal Co-operation of Colored Ministers.

Another striking factor in the church life of the community is the informal co-operation that has grown up between some of the colored ministers of the Baptist, Methodist and Episcopal churches. On more than one occasion during past years, when group interests of the Negro population have been involved, they have conferred, resolved and acted together. There has been difference of opinion in the community as to the final wisdom of their action. But the important point is that they acted together and after consultation and agreement.

From this fact another was observed and partially corroborated. There is no strong denominational difference emphasized among Negro churchmen in this Northern city. Some Negro new-comers from the South may not have lived long enough in such an atmosphere to be so free from strong denominational bias. They, however, will probably catch some of the more liberal spirit with broad-minded leadership.

Cordial Relations of White and Colored Church Leaders.

The cordial attitude and relation of the white and colored church leaders is another fact of prime importance. The white Baptist ministers have welcomed the leading colored Baptist ministers into their ministers' meetings. The fraternal relations of the Episcopal clergy have been equally cordial. No testimony was secured on this point from other denominations, but there is every reason to believe that similar hands of brotherly fellowship would be extended.

On every hand, white leaders of the several denominations testified to a general interest among laymen and clergy in the growing religious and community needs of their brothers of color. They expressed a willingness to help on any practical, constructive plan that might promise results.

In order that the detailed facts reported from the several churches may be examined, the table which follows is added. The investigator needs to repeat that the statements embodied in the table are such as were furnished him. There was time or opportunity to verify only some of the sources. Table III. with the details follows:

Table III.—Showing Size, Equipment and Location of Ten Principal Negro Churches by Name and Denominations in Detroit, Michigan, 1917

Name and Denomination.	Organized.	Reported Value of Church and Land.	Reported Value of Parsonage and Other Property of Church.	Reported Indebtedness Dec., 1917.	Total Reported Membership on Roll of Church.	Reported Enrolled in Sunday School.	Reported Enrolled in Young People's Societies.	Reported Financial Support Raised by Church the Past Year.	Reported Amount Paid on Improvements Past Year.	Reported Amount Paid on Indebtedness Last Year.	Reported Amount of Salary of Minister Raised by Church.	Other Items Furnished Minister by Church.
Second Baptist	1836	$50,000	$5,000		1900	759	400	$12,360	$2,361	$10,000, including running expenses	$1,800	House, fuel, light, telephone, private secretary
St. Matthews Protestant Episcopal	1846	$25,000—$30,000	$16,000	$8,400	512	125 main 30 mission	(all girls) 52	$5,600 to Dec. 23, 1917	$300—$506	$1,600	$1,500	House, fuel, light, telephone
Bethel A. M. E.	May, 1841	$40,000	$14,000	$7,000	2170	300	100	Unknown	Unknown	$2,000	$1,800	House, fuel, light, telephone
Ebenezer A. M. E.	May, 1887	$20,000	$7,000	$1,000	740	250	75	$8,900	$150	$3,500 mortgage	$1,500	House, fuel, light, telephone
Macedonia Baptist	April, 1917	(including other property) $30,000 (?)		$9,500	Started with 5, now, 826	76	86	Eight months $2,550.35	$500	$500	$1,200	Parsonage in rear
Scott M. E.	1912	$6,000	None	$1,260	432	246	72	$2,200	$564	$300	$1,460	
A. M. E. Zion	1903	$3,000	None	None	150	60	25			$1,900	$800	
St. John C. M. E.	July, 1917	$20,000 (?)	$7,000 (?)	$12,000	167	50	30	$4,000	Since July, 1917. $3,300 on both debt & improvements			
Shiloh Baptist	Sept., 1913	$9,000 including rooms upstairs for parsonage,		$5,000 Purchase mortgage	250	90	60—70	$2,000	$1,700 on present property—amount came from sale of other site	$2,000	$65 mo.	Apartments, fuel, light, telephone
St. Peters, A. M. E Zion-Hamtramck	1910	$3,500	None	$2,500	90	35	20	$400	$700 both on improvements and debt		?	

CHAPTER V.

General Summary and Recommendations

During the past two years Detroit's Negro population has increased from about 6,000 to between 20,000 and 25,000. The new-comers are mainly from the Southern states, especially Alabama, Georgia, Florida, and Tennessee. The majority have been crowded into a Negro district which had been formed and had become partly segregated before their arrival. They have expanded this district. Some have found homes also in several smaller neighborhoods in the western and northwestern parts of the city and in a suburb continuous with the city limits. There is an evident division of the new-comers from the older residents.

There is a large industrial demand from Detroit manufacturers for Negro laborers. The greater part of this demand is for unskilled workers, although probably as high as 10 per cent. of the calls was for semi-skilled and skilled workers. There is among some employers divergence of opinion about Negro workers. Some complaints have been made relative to the Negro's slowness, irregularity, and disinclination to work out of doors when cold weather comes, yet thousands of Negro workmen are employed and scores of firms are ready to employ more of them. The satisfaction they are giving must be considerable. The success of experiments in employing colored women in a garment factory and as ushers in a theatre gives indications of another source of income for the group. These facts indicate that the industrial demand will probably be constant and a large population permanently settled in the city. There is need for enlarging the employment finding facilities and for vocational training for men and women.

The housing conditions have been very poor. Rents are excessive, the increase has been estimated by one observer from 50 per cent. to 350 per cent. in some cases during the past eighteen months. This made it necessary probably for the majority of new-comers to take lodgers into their homes. Overcrowding was thus increased and other family dangers added. Here is a great need.

DIAGRAM — *Showing comparative number of saloons, pool-rooms, gambling clubs, and churches in the district where the largest number of Negroes live, Detroit, 1917*

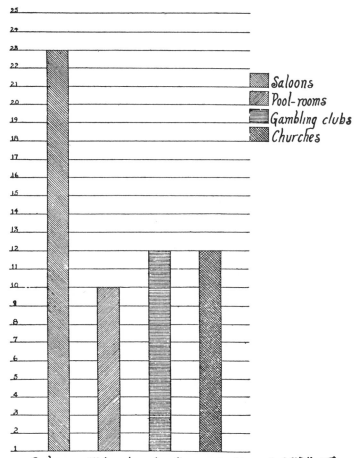

Saloons will be closed after next May, but "Blind Tigers" are known to have followed in other cities

Some good beginnings have been made to provide whole-some recreation through baseball, football, and basketball leagues, through inducing the recreation commission to open one of the high schools gymnasia and through a community dance in one of the public schools. For girls, a Camp Fire and for boys a company of Boy Scouts have been started.

There are five colored Protestant churches with good buildings, strong membership, and fine leadership. There are five other colored Protestant churches which are doing very well. Five additional struggling colored Protestant churches were definitely located. With two or three exceptions, all the denominations with any considerable Negro membership are represented. Baptists and Methodists naturally have the largest number of Negro communicants in Detroit. Only three churches, two of them organized in 1917, reported any indebtedness. They show a large amount of initiative and possible financial resources. The problem, then, is not so much the establishment of new churches as it is the development of efficiency in the existing ones.

The emphatic testimony of Mr. Forrester B. Washington, director of the Detroit Urban League, is that in placing about 10,000 Negro workers, those who come through the churches or who had church attachments were the most dependable and satisfactory. The relation of the churches to the recreation and amusement problem has been one of informal co-operation.

There is a fine, brotherly relationship among the colored ministers. The emphasis on denominational differences was conspicuous by its absence. An excellent relationship of co-operation exists between the white and colored churchmen. On every hand, the denominational leaders of white people expressed the opinion that their fellow members were interested and would co-operate on a practical, constructive program.

PROPOSED PROGRAM

1. The Challenge to White and Colored Churches of Detroit.

Co-operation should be the slogan for the community movement. It should be clearly understood that the churches were made for the people and not the people for the churches. The most evident fact operating to offset the fullest community co-operation is the division of the old colored residents and the new-comers and a lack of consciousness of common community interests between white and colored people. To replace this condition by one of co-operative citizenship and interest in one's fellows, however humble, is the great end sought. In other words, the Christ spirit of neighborliness should be infused into all the community activities.

This is being done as effectively as present circumstances permit by the pastors and leading citizens, white and colored, by their joint service in the newly organized community activities and in the informal co-operation of the churches of the several denominations.

But the need is larger than the present available forces can meet now. It is pressing and challenges both the local churches and the denominational church mission Boards. This need divides itself into two parts. First, the need of assimilating these new-comers into the life of the community on such matters as obtaining work, training workers in efficiency; the improvement of housing, the provision of recreation facilities, and the like.

Second, the need of more well equipped churches for the new-comers where the ethical and social ideals of the Christ may be presented and rehearsed to give the motive power for clean living and wholesome citizenship.

Considering the social needs, the churches have a challenge to secure or train in spirit and technique men and women of vision to assist in the exacting, executive and administrative work which the joint community organization, proposed below, should undertake. The expansion of work in employment placement, training courses for those employed, recreation, and the like will require much more executive supervision than the present available workers could handle.

The churches have a challenge in the need of a community house in the Negro district. This is partly a call for money. Such a house should be undenominational in character. It should be a neutral meeting ground for all the community activities among Negroes. There is also large need for financial support to pioneer the providing of facilities and teachers for vocational classes for untrained adult workers. Women in large numbers need such instruction now to make them employable.

In meeting the church needs, some of the present churches might be judiciously aided to become well equipped, and they should be used to their capacity. New churches will probably be needed soon, but these should be encouraged only after careful study of the people's needs, especially as the gradual Negro population centers shift, as well as those of other groups, making some of the present church sites useless and calling for new ones.

The recreation movements now started would be greatly increased in effectiveness by the active help of the churches. Every Sunday School and young people's society in the colored churches could have its baseball team, its football team, and its basketball team. A city league of such teams could readily be formed under some neutral supervision. Contests and tournaments would follow with the seasons.

There is sore need of greater support from the churches in the community effort to provide other wholesome recreation and amusement. The moving pictures and poolrooms need censoring and supervision. Other activities need guidance.

Let the churches recognize that the routine modern city life and industry demand these diversions to break the monotony. Let the churches furnish the guiding ideals!

One of the objects of this proposed plan of co-operative organization should be to seek and encourage the coming to the city of competent religious leaders. Such a plan would serve to help secure financial support for needed churches and other worthy religious agencies. It should serve also to discourage ill advised churches and projects as well as help to protect the giving public from religious charlatans.

Finally, the churches are challenged to furnish the Christian men and women and the larger Christ ideals as motive power for service on boards of the institutions, and social agencies of the Negro community, and for creating that public opinion which will make possible the larger life to Negro citizens.

A general neutral organization formed on some plan of co-operation of the social agencies and the churches might well be attempted. The present organization of the Detroit Urban League formed by representatives from a number of social agencies might be enlarged by some plan as to give the churches, white and colored, opportunity for a more active and responsible part in the plans for helping the new-comers. The local leaders are best able to work out a suitable plan of organization for such co-operation. The opinions of a number of white and colored leaders both in the church and social work leaves the impression that some such neutral organization would be welcomed and find support.

2. *The Challenge to the Denominational Mission Boards.*

The solution of the problems due to the Negro migration to Detroit and other Northern cities is a challenge to the church to apply the principles of the Christ to a concrete religious and social situation. Therefore, it seems to the writer that there rests upon the Christian statesmen of the Mission Boards the responsibility of guiding the churches toward that solution.

First, Detroit probably needs a thoroughly social survey following this preliminary one. The survey might be extended if adequately financed to other urban centres. It might be done in co-operation with some social agencies. But this challenge, like that to the churches of Detroit, calls for co-operative action. (The selection of denominational representatives for the colored work with all the duplication it implies, it seems to the writer, might be going in the wrong direction).

Second, we all recognize that a study of the situation is only a means to an end. That end should be such constructive work as a survey might propose for the development of the new-comers into Christian citizens. Cannot the denominational Boards co-operate in support of workers in the field? Would it not be a strategic step to put a man in Detroit?

3. *First Steps in the Proposed Plan.*

The Detroit forces might be increased now by putting a colored man in the field to help carry the heavy work such as a co-operative church and community organization would necessarily be called upon to do. If sent, he should not be independent of any existing staff of colored social workers, but might be a regular part of it. He might be given every opportunity to move slowly and be of help, not a hindrance through acts taken on half knowledge of the church and community conditions. He might be sent to Detroit in the spirit of Christian service to do a constructive, co-operative work. He should have plenty of time, say a year, to get his bearings and begin to know the good people of Detroit. He should learn from those on the ground how to help. He would come to understand the

39

local situation of all the religious bodies—Protestant, Catholic, and Jewish—for communicants of all these faiths are doing something to help the Negro new-comers.

The work such a man might do would demonstrate not for Detroit alone. It would be an example soon copied in other cities having the problems of the new-comers. What might be the work of such a man?

1. He could assume a share of the executive work of the several lines of community improvement, such as housing, recreation, health, or other activities that might be started by the organizations.

2. He could organize and conduct social work classes of intelligent laymen in the churches and Sunday-Schools.

3. He could assist the churches in a study of their membership and their neighborhoods.

4. He could assist in supervising and directing volunteer workers whom the churches would inspire.

The gift of the churches has been the spirit of Christ. The churches should be witnessing to this spirit through service of their members to the new-comers, active in doing their share in all good community work, whether called a religious organization or not. The work should testify to the Christ because the work was done by the Christ spirit in individuals. The Negro new-comers to Northern cities are a new challenge to Christian statesmanship.

BIBLIOGRAPHY ON NEGRO MIGRATION.

ABBOTT, (Edith) and BRECKINRIDGE, (S. P.):

Housing Conditions in Chicago, No. VI.—The Problem of the Negro. By A. B. Cornstock. Reprints from the Journal of Sociology. Vol. XVIII., No. 2. Scientific, reliable, sympathetic.

DuBois, W. E. B.:

The Philadelphia Negro. Ginn and Company, Boston. First able, scholarly study of the city Negro.

DANIEL, John:

In Freedom's Birthplace. Houghton-Mifflin Co., Boston. A well seasoned study of the Boston Negro.

EPSTIEN, Abraham:

The Negro Migrant in Pittsburgh. A study in Social Economics (Illustrated). Published under the supervision of the School of Economics, University of Pittsburgh. A good study of the facts; especially sympathetic and impartial. Amateurish in analysis and arrangement.

HAYNES, George E.:

The Negro at Work in New York City—Columbia University Studies in History, Economics and Public Law. Vol. XLIX., No. 3. A study of the manner and causes of migration of Negroes to the cities, North and South, 1860 to 1910, with special material about New York City.

HAYNES, George E.:

Conditions Among Negroes in the Cities. Article in Annals of the American Academy of Political and Social Science. Vol. XLIX., pp. 105-119, September, 1913. Also articles on migration in the Survey, Vol. 39, April and June, 1918.

MOSES, Kingsley:

The Negroes Come North. Article in the Forum, Vol. LVIII., No. 2, pp. 181-190, August, 1917. A cursory discussion of little information value.
Negro, The, in the Cities of the North. Charities (now Survey), Vol. 15, No. 1, October, 1915. Informing, popular articles.

Reports:

Annual reports of the following organizations:

a. National League on the Urban Conditions Among Negroes for 1916 and 1917. Address 2303 17th Avenue, New York.

b. Chicago League on Urban Conditions Among Negroes. For the Fiscal Year Ended October 31, 1917. Address 3303 South State Street, Chicago.

c. Armstrong Association of Philadelphia, 1917. Endorsed by Philadelphia Chamber of Commerce. Affiliated with the National League on Urban Conditions Among Negroes.

d. The Public Welfare League, Nashville, Tenn., 708 Cedar Street.

ROSE, John C.:

Movements of Negro Population as Shown by Census of 1910. Article in American Economic Review, Vol. IV, No. 2, pp. 281-292, June, 1914.

United States Census Bureau, Washington:

Bulletin 8, Twelfth Census Negroes in the United States, pp. 11-68. Bulletin 129, Thirteenth Census Negroes in the United States, pp. 7-15.

United States Report of the Industrial Commission, Vol. XIX., Sections on testimony relating to migration during reconstruction. Superintendent of Documents, Washington, D. C.

THE NEGRO
IN WASHINGTON

Prepared by Sterling Brown
for the Federal Writers' Project

THE NEGRO
IN WASHINGTON

★

THE history of Washington so far sketched has been a chronicle of events from the city's distant beginnings to its indelible present, concerning itself mainly with the white population. But the story would remain incomplete without a discussion of the Negro in Washington who, from the start, exerted a profound influence upon the city's destiny. Aside from the fact that at the present day the Negro population constitutes more than one-fourth of the city's total, the Negro's subtler influences are by far greater than might be apparent on the surface.

Chronologically this subject lends itself to treatment in three distinct periods.

I. FROM THE BEGINNINGS TO THE CIVIL WAR

Benjamin Banneker, a Negro mathematician, was appointed by George Washington to serve on Major L'Enfant's commission for the surveying and laying out of the city. Though this might be considered symbolic of the Negro's later participation in Washington life, the lot of Banneker's fellows, even in our times, has hardly been so auspicious. Viewing Washington in its early years Thomas Moore found

> Even here beside the proud Potowmac's streams . . .
> The medley mass of pride and misery
> Of whips and charters, manacles and rights
> Of slaving blacks and democratic whites . . .

Though spoken by a pro-British son of Erin, his indictment is substantiated by other sources.

It was not alone the shabby contrast between the profession of democracy and the practice of slavery that struck the observer, nor was it chiefly the brutality of the working and living conditions of slaves in the District of Columbia. Although conditions hardly deserved to be called ideal, still the cook, coachman, and artisan, in Alexandria, Georgetown, or Washington, or the truck-farmer in the rural areas surrounding these towns was generally better off than the field hand in the deep South and Southwest. What brought ill-fame to the District was the extensive slave trading conducted here. Because of its location, the District served as a natural outlet for both the coastwise slave ships and the overland coffles and was rightly called the very seat and center of the domestic slave traffic.

The District of Columbia, too small for slave rearing itself, served as depot for the purchases of interstate traders, who combed Maryland and northern Virginia for slaves. Since the slave jails, colloquially known as "Georgia pens", and described by an ex-slave as worse than hog holes, were inadequate for the great demand, the public jails were made use of, accommodations for criminals having to wait upon the more pressing and lucrative traffic in slaves. There were pens in what is now Potomac Park; and one in the Decatur House, fronting on what is now Lafayette Square. More notorious were McCandless' Tavern in Georgetown; in Washington, Robey's Tavern at Seventh and Maryland Avenue, and Williams' "Yellow House" at Eighth and B Streets SW. In Alexandria, the pretentious establishment of Armfield and Franklin, who by 1834 were sending more than a thousand slaves a year to the Southwest, was succeeded and surpassed by the shambles of the much-feared Kephart.

In 1819, when Miller's Tavern at Thirteenth and F Streets NW. was on fire, a bystander, William Gardiner, refused to join the customary bucket brigade and loudly denounced the place as a slave prison. The resulting controversy conducted in newspaper columns revealed the tragic past of the tavern. A Negro woman, about to be sold South apart from her husband, had leapt in frenzy from an attic window, breaking both arms and injuring her back, but surviving. This focused attention upon the local slave trade. Humanitarian Jesse Torrey came to Washington shortly after the attempted suicide, visited the injured woman, and discovered two kidnaped Negroes in the attic. He began suit in the circuit court for their freedom, the expenses being defrayed by a group of persons headed by Francis Scott Key, who gave his legal services gratis. It is highly probable that the stir attendant upon this celebrated case urged the slave owner John Randolph to that bitter invective in which he said:

You call this the land of liberty, and every day that passes things are done in it at which the despotisms of Europe would be horror-struck and disgusted.

. . . In no part of the earth—not even excepting the rivers on the Coast of Africa, was there so great, so infamous a slave market, as in the metropolis, in the seat of government of this nation which prides itself on freedom.

A chorus of voices rose in harmony with Randolph's. The sight recorded by Torrey, and engraved as the frontispiece of his *Portraiture of Domestic Slavery*, of a coffle of manacled slaves, like a butcher's drove of hobbled cattle, passing along the east front of the ruined Capitol, became a familiar figure in the many orations attacking the traffic. The struggle for abolition in the District recruited such men as Benjamin Lundy, Salmon P. Chase, Charles Miner, Charles Sumner, William Lloyd Garrison, Henry Wilson, William H. Seward, and Abraham Lincoln when serving as Congressman. John Quincy Adams' famous fight for free speech and against the "gag rule" in Congress was prompted by the refusal of the two Houses to hear petitions for the abolition of slavery in the District of Columbia. But the forces commanded by men like Calhoun were too great, and while solicitude was expressed by Northerners and Southerners, Congress, which had the power to abolish, refused to act. The District, wedged in between two slave States, was kept slave territory, and the slave trade prospered until the Compromise of 1850. The black code of the District was even more severe than the codes of Maryland and Virginia of which it was the reenactment, and the "stealing" of free Negroes was shamefully widespread. William Wells Brown, in *Clotel*, the first novel by a Negro, has one of his heroines jump into the Potomac to escape slave catchers.

The Negroes of Washington, both free and slave, at times took matters into their own hands against these flagrant abuses. The Underground Railroad had important stopping places in Washington; ex-slaves today remember churches whose basements served as layovers, and out-of-the-way Georgetown homes that were specially marked for the fugitives. One of the famous trails started at a cemetery skirting the stage road leading north from the city. It is probable that Harriet Tubman, "the Moses of her people", the greatest underground agent, worked around Washington as well as on the Eastern Shore. Legend has it that she was discovered by her friends asleep in a local park beneath a sign advertising a reward for her capture, which meant nothing to her, as she could not read.

In 1848, 77 Negroes under slave and free Negro leadership, took advantage of the relaxed patrolling of Washington while it was celebrating the liberty of the new French Republic, and escaped on board Captain Drayton's *Pearl*. But at Cornfield Harbor, 140 miles from Washington, contrary winds forced the schooner into

70

shelter and an armed steamer captured the runaways and the crew. The manner of flight had been betrayed by a Negro hackman. Captain Drayton was mobbed (an Irishman cutting off a piece of his ear), sentenced to a fine of $10,000, and imprisoned until Sumner prevailed upon President Fillmore to intercede. For captured Negroes there was only occasional intercession. Emily and Mary Edmondson, long coveted by the trader Bruin, were sold South, but later were redeemed through Henry Ward Beecher and other sympathizers. Another Emily, who had hoped to reach her mother in New York, met with a different fate. Said to be the "finest looking woman in this county", and destined as a "fancy article" for New Orleans, she died from exposure on the overland trek. Her mother, who had bought herself free by labors over the washtub, thanked God.

In 1830 there were 6,152 free Negroes in the District of Columbia compared with 6,119 slaves; in 1840, 8,361 compared with 4,694 slaves; and in 1860, 11,131 compared with only 3,185 slaves. Thus, in 30 years, the free colored population was nearly doubled, while the slave population was halved. It would be inaccurate to infer from this that there was any wholesale manumission or that the District was a haven for free Negroes. The free Negroes were of several classes: Those whose antecedents had never been slaves, such as descendants of indentured servants; those born of free parents, or of free mothers; those manumitted; those who had bought their own freedom, or whose kinsmen had bought it for them; and those who were successful runaways. These free Negroes were an ever present "bad example" to the slaves of the District and of the surrounding slave States, and the more they prospered, the "worse example" they became.

Especially stringent regulations affecting free Negroes were added by the District Common Council to the slave codes. Every free Negro was required: (1) to give the mayor "satisfactory evidence of freedom", plus $50 for himself, and $50 for each member of his family; (2) to post a bond for $1,000 and to secure five white guarantors of good behavior. It was necessary to show manumission papers in order to remain free; even so, gangs bent on kidnaping could and frequently did seize and destroy them. No Negro, slave or free, could testify against whites. The jails were crowded with captured free Negroes and suspected runaways; there were 290 of these in the city jail at one time. Many were sold for prison fees, ostensibly for a fixed period, but really for life. Meetings for any other than fraternal and religious purposes were forbidden. After

71

Nat Turner's insurrection in Virginia in 1831, colored preachers were banned. Curfew rang at 10 o'clock for all Negroes, free or slave.

In spite of all this the class of free Negroes increased and, in the main, advanced. Though forbidden by law to do so many succeeded, through the connivance of friendly whites, in opening and running such businesses as hotels, taverns, saloons, and restaurants. In the District, as in so many southern cities, they had a monopoly of barbering and free colored boys were porters and bootblacks. Waiters were numerous and, in the gay hospitality of a southern city, were comparatively well paid. There were many skilled carpenters, bricklayers, shoemakers, stonemasons, wheelwrights, blacksmiths, plasterers, printers, cabinetmakers, cab drivers, and draymen. For free colored women the opportunities were limited to dressmaking, laundry work, nursing, and general housework.

With chances for a livelihood scanty, many Negroes were driven to petty larceny. The newspapers, as is their custom, interpreted this frequently as grand larceny. The Old Center Market was the resort of plundering marauders. Many Negroes ignored or violated the laws, particularly the curfew. Race riots developed in spite of the fact that the penalty for striking a white man was the cropping of the ears (exacted in the District until 1862). Mulattoes sometimes set up invidious self-defeating distinctions against their darker brothers. Frequently the blacks retaliated. There were unfortunate examples of Negroes serving as informers, as catchers of runaways, as hat-in-hand seekers of personal favors, and ex-slaves still speak with hatred of one Stonestreet, a Negro slave-kidnaper. But more often there was co-operation, the Resolute Beneficial Society being founded for concerted action toward the betterment of conditions. Occasionally free Negroes owned slaves. However, they were usually wealthier Negroes buying kinsfolk for liberation.

The free Negro was avid for education. In 1807, shortly after the first two white schoolhouses had been built, three recently freed Negroes who could not read or write hired a white teacher and set up the first school for Negroes. More successful were the ventures of such pioneers as Louisa Parke Costin, Mary Wormley, Arabella Jones, Father Vanlomen, and Maria Becraft. John F. Cook, a shoemaker, set up a school in 1834, 8 years after his aunt, Alethia Tanner, had purchased his freedom. The Snow Riot gave a set of hoodlums the excuse for attacking his school. Cook fled to Pennsylvania, but returned a year later, doggedly intent upon his mission. Myrtilla

Miner, a white woman from New York, driven from place to place in the city in her attempt to establish a Negro school, finally purchased the entire square between what are now Nineteenth and Twentieth and M and O Streets. Harriet Beecher Stowe's donation of $1,000 helped her greatly in this purchase, and Johns Hopkins was one of the trustees. Her students were insulted and attacked by white men along the streets. The buildings were stoned and set afire. But Miss Miner stood her ground. Using some of their leisure time, she and Emily Edmondson (of the famous case of the *Pearl*) warned hoodlums of their mettle by firing pistols at a target in the yard.

The education of Negroes was frowned upon by the majority of whites in the District, especially after Nat Turner's famous uprising. Negroes paid taxes for the support of white schools, but received no consideration themselves. Private Negro schools continued to spring up and no school closed its doors for lack of "scholars." In 1860 there were more than 1,200 free colored children in school.

Church was the solace of the free Negroes. Negro Methodism in the District started in 1820 when a group of free Negroes withdrew from Ebenezer Church and formed a separate congregation. After 1831 when obvious discrimination started in most of the white churches, other Negro groups withdrew from congregations. At St. Johns Church an outside stairway leading to the gallery was called the "niggers' backstairs to heaven." But the Negro members decided that there must be other ways to get there and left the church. In 1833 the First Baptist Church, moving from Nineteenth and I Streets NW. to a new edifice which later became Ford's Theater, instituted segregation. Negro members stayed in the old home. One feature of the churches was the popularity of Sabbath schools among adults as well as among children because they furnished instruction in the three R's. Taking advantage of every chance, the free Negro frequently left Jonah waiting and the Walls of Jericho standing while he fathomed the mysteries of the alphabet.

The houses in which free Negroes lived ran the gamut from hovels to commodious homes. The first were remote from slave quarters, and crouched behind the imposing dwellings of employers, or were grouped in hidden alleyways. The homes of the well-to-do, scattered here and there, were purchased before the law forbidding free Negroes to own property was passed, or later in defiance of it. There were some separate communities, especially in Southwest Washington, "on the island" (so-called because the Tiber and the old canal cut it off from the city). Many free Negroes were poverty stricken, and gave point to the proslavery argument of the wretched freedman, but with the odds against them, it is surprising that this impoverished class was not larger. Many, comparatively wealthy, owned property in such a valuable section as Fifteenth and New York Avenue; many had homes on Sixteenth Street; and a feed dealer, Alfred Lee, purchased the mansion on H Street which had been the British Embassy. In 1865, when scoffers charged that Negroes did not own $40,000 worth of property in the whole city, it was proved that in one square their holdings aggregated $45,592. At the time of the Emancipation Act, Negroes in the District of Columbia were paying taxes on $650,000 worth of real estate.

II. FROM THE CIVIL WAR TO THE TURN OF THE CENTURY

In 1862, the year in which slavery was abolished in the District, President Lincoln authorized the enlisting of Negroes as part of the Army. Two regiments were soon mustered in from the District and vicinity, the First organized at Washington in May 1863, and the Second at Arlington a month later. These regiments served with honor at Fair Oaks, Petersburg, Fort Taylor, and in other battles. It is estimated that the District supplied over 3,000 colored troops of the 200,000 in the Union Army. Negro contrabands, male and female, had earlier crowded to the camps, eager to serve as teamsters and road builders, laundresses, and cooks for "Marse Lincum's boys."

As early as 1862 more than 13,000 refugees had collected in Washington, Alexandria, Hampton, and Norfolk. The Emancipation Proclamation in 1863 was an added stimulus to Negroes to flee to the Union lines. Washington, strategically located for slave trading. now became the favorite place toward which contrabands headed. The mustering out of Negro regiments in Washington at the close of the war further increased their number in the District. Washington became a Mecca for Negroes in the next two decades, and in 1880 there were 59,696 in the city and its immediate environs. The proportion to the city's population (about one-third) remained fairly constant.

The picture therefore is greatly changed from what it had been in 1867, when one-fifth of all owners of real estate had been Negroes. In the main the refugees were illiterate and penniless. At their best, these people were intelligent and eager to help themselves; at their worst they showed, in the words of a Federal chaplain, "cringing deceit, theft, licentiousness, all the vices which slavery inevitably fosters." They constituted a grave problem for the District. One proposed way out was colonization. President Lincoln favored this, and Congress appropriated funds for transportation to Liberia or Haiti. Several hundred former slaves were shipped to the Island of Vache, Haiti. But when their plight became desperate, a war-ship was sent after them. They were settled in Arlington in a place known as "Freedmen's Village", very near a tract left by George Washington Parke Custis to his colored daughter, Maria Syphax. Appeals were made to encourage Negroes to migrate en masse to sections farther north, or to return to the plantations in the South. But the majority chose to remain in Washington.

The first contrabands during the war were housed in the old "Brick Capitol", on the site of the present Supreme Court Building. They were then moved to what was Duff Green's Row, east of the Capitol. As the flood swept in, McClellan's Barracks housed them, and then numerous barracks were built in Washington and Alexandria. Two hundred tenements were fitted up at Campbell Hospital. Many Negroes settled in the neighborhoods of the old forts. The Fort Reno settlement in Tenleytown is one of the last of these to succumb to fine suburban developments. In the main, how-ever, philanthropic efforts did not prove equal to the housing short-age. Real-estate agents floated a project that resulted in Washing-ton's notorious "alley system." The deep back yards, and even the front yards provided by L'Enfant's plan, were found to promise more alluring rewards than lovely gardens. Lots were divided and the rear portions sold separately. The first of the ill-fated alleys, as the present day Washington knows them, were laid out in 1867. In 1897 there were 333 alleys, inhabited by approximately 19,000 people, more than three-fourths of them Negroes. Shacks costing as little as $10 proved highly profitable investments. Here, in these disease-infested sties, ex-slaves got their first taste of freedom. And it is here that, in too large numbers, their children's children still drag out their lives.

Negro communities had such suggestive names as Goose Level, Vinegar Hill, Froggy or Foggy Bottom, Hell's Bottom, Swampoodle, and Bloodfield. Cowtown, so-called because, outside of the city proper, cows and hogs and chickens ranged at will on sidewalks and streets, was the present Barry Place. Of a somewhat higher level were the communities across the Anacostia: The Flats, Hills-dale, Barry Farms (an earlier settlement of race-conscious slaves), Stantonstown, Garfield; those in the northeast at Benning, and Burrville; and Brightwood, in the vicinity of Fort Stevens and Fort Slocum. Georgetown had its goodly share of oldest inhabitants, who sat aloof, gazing with well-bred disdain at the ignorant trespassers. Other prosperous Negroes were scattered in almost all of the quiet residential sections.

For new arrivals, accustomed chiefly to manual labor in the fields, there was little employment to be found in a city predominantly governmental and residential. Pauperism forced many to eke out a living by pickings on the dumps. Many took to pilfering. It is hardly a matter of wonder that the rate of crime was high. The paths of many Negroes led straight from the alley to the workhouse. Crimes of violence were numerous. In 1891 the superintendent of police attributed much of the crime to the neglected state of the Negro child. Illegitimacy was frequent. Health conditions were wretched. The death rate in 1891 for Negroes was nearly double that for whites, and both were far too high. The death rate was largely increased by infant mortality. In spite of all this, Negroes were unwilling to go to the poorhouse. Perhaps they saw no reason merely to change addresses.

And yet the grimness of the picture is not without some relief. The Freedmen's Bureau, missionary organizations, and Negroes themselves with their lodges, churches, and schools, waged a determined though hard-pressed battle against prejudice, poverty, and ignorance. The Freedmen's Bureau was created by act of Congress in 1865, for "relief work, education, regulation of labor, and administration of justice", among the freedmen. Major General Oliver Otis Howard, who had lost an arm at Fair Oaks but had returned to serve under Sherman and as commander of the Army of Tennessee, was named commissioner. Unable to cope successfully, for all its gallant efforts, with the problems of destitution and housing, the Freedmen's Bureau exerted its greatest influence in the establishing of Freedmen's Hospital, Howard University, and a number of schools for Negroes that eventually became a part of the city school system. Some of the officials of the Bureau were connected with the Freedmen's Savings and Trust Company which, contrary to the opinions of some, was never controlled by Negroes. This company did not withstand the contagion of the Gilded Age. With its central bank in Washington and 34 branches in the South, it "received in the aggregate deposits amounting to $57,000,000 from more than 70,000 depositors, chiefly Negroes." It taught valuable lessons in thrift, but when, following the panic of 1873, the imprudence of its investments and the dishonesty of certain directors forced it to close its doors, it taught the freedmen an embittering lesson.

Although an act of Congress ruled that Washington and Georgetown should allocate to the trustees of colored schools a proportionate part of all moneys received, the corporation of Washington refused to do this as late as November 1867. After this Negro schools fared well. The northern missionary associations which had conducted schools in temporary barracks and basements of churches joined forces. A high school was organized in 1870. One of its frequent removals found it in Myrtilla Miner's famous building. Then in 1891, M Street High School was erected. Night schools, privately maintained for day-time workers, became part of the public-school system in 1886. George F. T. Cook, son of the militant educator John F. Cook, was appointed superintendent of schools in 1868. A heated contest was waged in 1871 under the leadership of William H. A. Wormley and William Syphax to remove all restrictions of color from the public schools, but those opposing segregation were defeated by whites and some Negroes who feared that mixed schools would return the issue to local politics, and mean the death of the progressing schools.

The old Negro preacher in Georgetown who said of the freed Negro: "Fifteen years after he came out of slavery, what did he do? Sat down by the River of Babylon and sang, 'Peace at home and pleasure abroad', and went to sleep down by the weeping willows for 25 years", was overstating the case. There was definite, if gradual economic advance. Many made their living as domestics, barbers, cobblers, grocers, dry-goods merchants, artisans, contractors, real-estate operators, hucksters, market vendors, saloonkeepers, and hotel-keepers. Others inherited property, made prudent investments, and became prosperous. Colored firemen were appointed on a full-time basis in 1870; colored policemen have been on the force since the Metropolitan Police was organized in the sixties. A colored policeman arrested General Grant for speeding; whether the culprit had set his people free or not, the law was the law.

At Fifteenth and H Streets stood one of Washington's most exclusive hotels, catering to family patronage and the congressional and diplomatic sets. This was owned and managed by a Negro, Wm. Wormley, close friend of Charles Sumner. Many Negroes found employment in the Government service, most of them as laborers, messengers, a few as clerks. Certain political plums fell to Negroes such as the positions of the fourth Auditor, the Register of the Treasury, and the Recorder of Deeds. There was an increasing professional class of doctors, lawyers, preachers, and teachers. Professors were ubiquitous, professors of music, of the dance, of the cakewalk, of algebra, and of penmanship. The title is not so comic when one recalls how rarely a Negro is granted the title "Mister."

Though politically well informed and articulate, the Negro of Washington in this period exerted little force. His newly acquired suffrage was swept away by the disfranchisement of the District in 1874, an act which was definitely influenced by the fact that Negroes comprised one-fourth of the population. Political figures among them, however, were numerous. There were over a score of Congressmen, many intelligent and able. Those whose imprint was most lasting upon Negro history were Robert Brown Elliott, John M. Langston, and John R. Lynch, who later corrected many of Rhodes' inaccuracies in reconstruction history. Representative Ransier caused a commotion during one session while John T. Harris of Virginia was declaiming: "And I say that there is not one gentleman upon this floor who can honestly say that he really believes that the colored man is created his equal." Ransier interrupted with a casual "I can." Later, Ransier, listening to a Negro-baiter who insisted that the Civil Rights Bill meant that Negroes would absorb the whites, stated with suavity that "If we are powerful, we know how to be merciful." Negro Senators were Hiram R. Revels and Blanche Kelso Bruce, both of Mississippi. P. B. S. Pinchback, after a picaresque career culminating in the lieutenant governorship of Louisiana, and Francis Cardoza, State treasurer of South Carolina, were prominent newcomers. Finally there was Frederick Douglass, justly famed fugitive and antislavery orator, later Marshal and Recorder of Deeds for the District, and Minister to Haiti, who spent his last years in the old Van Hook Mansion on Cedar Hill.

The Republican Party was favored in these years. Frederick Douglass' statement: "The Republican Party is the ship, all else the sea", was held axiomatic to such a degree, that when at the Second Baptist Lyceum (a free forum) a paper endorsing the Democrats followed one endorsing the Republicans, the audience hissed; newspapers called it "double play", and the chairman was accused of traitorous intentions against the entire Negro race. The most exciting political campaigns were contests for delegates to the Republican National Convention. The Blaine Invincible Republican Club and the W. Calvin Chase Republican Club were elaborately organized. The Cleveland administration, however, left not a few Negro Democrats in its wake.

For many years after the Civil War, Washington was said, with some justice, to have "the most distinguished and brilliant assemblage of Negroes in the world." The reputation was sustained by cultural societies such as the Second Baptist Lyceum, the Congressional Lyceum, and the Bethel Literary Society. The National Negro Academy had upon its rosters such scholars as W. E. B. DuBois, of Atlanta, the Grimke brothers, W. S. Scarborough, J. W. Cromwell, and Kelly Miller. At the close of the century Paul Laurence Dunbar, best-known Negro writer, lived here. From 1897 to 1898 he was assistant to another Negro, Daniel Murray, who held a high place in the Congressional Library. Dunbar wrote and gave readings of his poetry, reciting with gusto of the Negro peasant. Will Marion Cook, similarly distinguished in music, collaborator with Dunbar in such musical shows as *Clorindy* and *In Dahomey*, was for a number of years a resident of Washington. The two leading Negro newspapers of the period, W. Calvin Chase's Washington *Bee* ("Watch the Sting") and E. E. Cooper's *Colored American*, are not only valuable as indices to social life, but also refreshing because of the occasional highly personal combats between the editors.

Despite the destitution and the earnest fight to keep the grudged gains, there was still a gay social life for some Washington Negroes. Negro lodges were convivial as well as "mutually benevolent." Conventions of elders and bishops made Washington their Mecca. G. A. R. encampments in Washington gave excuses for lavish hospitality. The Emancipation Day ceremonies were for a long time popular turnouts, until rivalries terminated them. Two rival factions, urged by President Cleveland to reconcile their grievances, persisted in holding parades with brass bands and "queens of love and beauty" for each. The celebration did not survive this contretemps. Inaugural balls for Negroes, held on March 5 after the official ball, were likewise causes for dissension between groups claiming to represent Negro Washington. Other balls and banquets were numerous and prodigal in the dozens of hotels, buffet-cafes, and saloons. Churches and clubs had frequent excursions down the river to Marshall Hall, Notley Hall, and Chapel Point. There was a flamboyant sporting life; political dignitaries at times had to yield to a visitor like Peter Jackson, heavyweight champion of Australia, against whom John L. Sullivan drew the color line, or Isaac Murphy, noted Negro jockey of the eighties. Major Taylor, "the champion colored bicycle racer of the world", defended his title and, in spite of foul play, defeated all comers at the old Washington Coliseum.

Before the Civil War the elder Joseph Jefferson, lessee of the Washington Theater, had petitioned the city fathers to change the curfew law, as it affected "a great proportion of our audience of this [Negro] caste" and lessened his box-office receipts. This interest in drama persisted into the period under consideration. Musicals were very popular. A Negro opera company founded in 1872 gave several performances at Ford's Theater. Williams and Walker and Cole and Johnson, "in the brightest ebony offering, *A Trip to Coontown*", were viewed by Washington Negroes with only occasional disputes with the theater management over the sale of orchestra tickets. Sissieretta Jones, "Black Patti", sang in 1892 for President Harrison's White House reception; she returned in 1900 with her troubadours in *The Essence of Ole Virginny*. The biggest musical event in years was the first all-colored oratorio, *Emmanuel*, directed by Prof. J. Henry Lewis. He was versatile enough to train a chorus of 70 for "A Mammoth Cake Walk and Jubilee Entertainment in Convention Hall." The Fisk Jubilee Singers and other school choruses sang in Washington to raise funds for their institutions. Some musical organizations were the Dvorák Musical Association, the Amphion Glee Club, the Washington Permanent Chorus, and the Georgetown Musical Association.

III. THE TWENTIETH CENTURY

The first decade of the twentieth century was marked by a consolidation of some of the gains and a loss of others. Negro leaders, attracted by the period's visions of reform, turned more hopefully to the "race problem." In 1903 at Lincoln Temple Congregational Church there was a conference on "How to Solve the Race Problem." Suggested solutions were the setting up of a forty-ninth state, the conciliatory gradualism of Booker T. Washington, and the demanding of full citizenship rights. It was urged that a "Commission to Consider Every Phase of the American Race Problem" be appointed by Congress, and a "Permanent Commission on the American Race Problem" was set up. Many of the militant members of the conference, hardly to be satisfied with commissions and committees, later joined forces with liberal movements which in 1910 culminated in the National Association for the Advancement of Colored People.

With America's entry into the World War, advice came from Negro leadership to forget grievances and close ranks for the sake of democracy. In Washington this was enthusiastically heeded. The First Separate Battalion, the Negro National Guard unit, which had previously served on the Mexican border, was called upon to guard Washington. This battalion was the first in the District to be mustered to war strength. Its commanding officer, Maj. James Walker, was the first District officer to die in the line of duty. When the Three Hundred and Seventy-second Regiment was formed, the First Separate Battalion was included. Overseas this regiment was brigaded with the "Red Hand" Division of the French Army. Of nearly 600 Washington Negroes in the outfit, more than 200 were wounded and 33 killed. One of the first to fall fatally wounded was Private Kenneth Lewis, a mere youngster, just out of the high-school cadet corps. He was awarded the *Medaille Militaire*. A score of Washingtonians received the *Croix de Guerre*, and the Three Hundred and Seventy-second Regiment had its colors deco-rated with the *Croix de Guerre* and palm for distinguished service.

In October 1917 Emmett J. Scott was appointed by Newton Baker as Special Assistant to the Secretary of War, in order to promote "a healthy morale among Negro soldiers and civilians." Attempts were made in his office to iron out cases of discrimination and in-justice. A campaign was zealously initiated to obtain a separate training camp for Negro officers, since no Negro, regardless of quali-fications, was permitted to enter the other camps. The spearhead of this movement was found in the newly established office and at Howard University. After much hesitation, authorization of a camp at Des Moines, Iowa, came on May 19, 1917. It is perhaps more than a coincidence that four days earlier, Henry Johnson and Needham Roberts, enlisted Negroes of the Fifteenth New York, had performed feats of valor for which they were later cited by General Pershing. From Des Moines 700 commissioned officers were sent out, the majority to serve in the Ninety-second Combat Division. Many were Washingtonians and of these several were cited for bravery, especially in the Argonne offensive. Over 5,000 Negroes from the District came into service through the operation of the selective draft law. World War veterans were organized in the James Reese Europe Post No. 5, and the James E. Walker Post No. 26 of the American Legion.

The hopes expressed "that the American people will be disposed more and more to remove such handicaps and to right such injustices as we now struggle against after the settlement of this great emer-gency which now faces our common country" turned barren in the post-war years. A bloody riot had taken place in East St. Louis during the war; on July 19, 1919, the Washington riot started. In-flammatory headlines announced a wave of assaults on white women by Negroes; several of these earlier publicized attacks were shown to be false, and later ones were definitely invented as whips for the mob. A number of white soldiers, sailors, and marines proceeded to southwest Washington and beat up several innocent Negroes.

Negroes retaliated and beat up several innocent whites. Street fighting was fierce, if sporadic. On July 21 a newspaper announced a "mobilization of every available service man stationed in or near Washington or on leave . . . the purpose is a clean-up." Negroes mobilized likewise, alley dwellers and most respectable burghers, side by side, and there was no clean-up. The bitter resistance of Negroes, the calling out of regular troops (officially this time), and a rainstorm helped the authorities to disperse the mobs. A year later, a Negro charged with murder confessed to the attacks for which two Negroes (positively identified by the women in the cases) were serving undeserved long-term sentences in penitentiaries.

The great forces opposed to the Negro, however, were not mobs that could be stopped at a brick barricade at Seventh and M Streets. These were, as they have always been, poverty, ignorance, disease, and crime. The extensive migration from the South, accelerated in the years of the war because of the cutting off of European immigration, the demand for industrial labor in the North and Midwest, and a growing resentment at conditions in the South, stranded many Negroes in Washington. Other cities were prepared for the mass invasion of industry, but Washington, even though it was growing

ALLEY DWELLERS IN WASHINGTON

by leaps and bounds, had little work for the newcomers to do. There was an aggravation of the post-Civil War problems of housing, health, and employment. At the collapse of the boom period, Negroes preferred the word "panic", depression being what they had experienced in the days of "prosperity."

Negroes of Washington total 27 percent of the population. At one time as many as 4 out of 10 were unemployed. Over 70 percent of the relief cases in 1935 were Negro, almost in inverse ratio to the racial distribution of the population. Many of these unemployed live in the 200 alleys which remain in the slum sections of Washington. An Alley Dwelling Elimination Act was enacted June 12, 1934, contemplating the riddance of inhabited alleys before July 1, 1944. Until then it is likely that these alley dwellings, for which exorbitant rents are charged, will continue to breed vice, crime, and disease.

Negroes who are able to make a living do so generally in domestic and personal service, and in manufacturing and mechanical pursuits (generally unskilled labor). A large number are in various departments under Civil Service; only a few of them, in spite of their capabilities, ranking as clerks or foremen. About 4,000 are listed in trade, and about 3,500 in the professions. The New Negro Alliance was founded in 1933 to demand equal working opportunity for Negroes in Negro areas. One of its slogans is "Don't Buy Where You Can't Work." But in spite of its picketing and boycotting, there has been no large gain in jobs. The struggling Negro business concerns cannot furnish much employment. Regardless of qualification, the Negro worker meets with definite discrimination. Many American Federation of Labor unions exclude him; even more than the white worker, he remains poorly led and unorganized. The Joint Committee on National Recovery, with headquarters in Washington, was active in focussing attention upon and fighting Nation-wide discrimination against, and exploitation of, Negroes.

Many of the slum streets are close seconds to the alleys in squalor, and a mushroom shanty-town at Marshall Heights on the outskirts of the city is much like the camp of the bonus-marchers, with "shelters" made out of pieces of tin, cast-off lumber and beaverboard. Prosperous Negroes live in all sections of the city and Negro expansion into areas of better homes has been bitterly, and at times unscrupulously, contested. "Covenants" to bar Negroes from certain sections were upheld by the Supreme Court in the Curtis case. But the "covenant", while a powerful weapon, frequently cuts both ways. During this century the fastnesses of Le Droit Park were penetrated

83

and transformed to a Negro section. Newer additions to Deanwood and Burrville in the northeast are Kingman Park, Capitol View, and De Priest Village, pleasing, well designed communities for the Negro middle class. Langston Terrace was sponsored by the Public Works Administration to afford better housing for Negro families of low income. The bulk of the Negro population, however, is still in the northwest, where the Negro business area is located.

The health situation resulting from the crowded slums is a grave menace. Only one city in the United States has a higher death rate from tuberculosis than Washington; over half of the tubercular cases in 1935 were Negroes. Other forces playing havoc are infant mortality, social diseases, accidents in the home, and disintegrated home life. Negro patients are received in segregated wards at most of the hospitals, while some of the hospitals afford clinic service only. Freedmen's Hospital, founded by the Freedmen's Bureau and supported by the Department of the Interior, is the Negro general hospital. Its facilities are utilized by the Howard University Medical School. There are also private hospitals conducted by leading surgeons of the race. Although in comparison with the rest of the country Washington has a heavy concentration of medical practitioners, the number is still not large enough to cope with the health problem. Recognition of the socio-economic causes of the high mortality rate is becoming more apparent in recent surveys and their resultant recommendations.

Crime is correspondingly high; areas found to be dense in disease are classed in police reports as dense in crime. Some alleys are "no man's land" for any stranger, Negro or white. Knives flash and pistols bark to terminate crap games and domestic brawls. Rasped nerves and short ugly tempers are not soothed by the heavy drinking of liquor which is as likely to be "canned heat" as corn whisky. Efforts of the police to ferret out crime are not helped by the furtiveness of the alley dwellers, who consider "John Law" to be their natural enemy—with good reason, at times, in light of police brutality. The "numbers" game, an American form of gambling, is popular in the alleys as it is on the avenues. The money that dribbles away to the number "baron" and "runner" could well be used for bread, milk, and shoes, but these poor people look upon the number slip as a magic sesame to momentary affluence.

Agencies struggling to improve these conditions are few in number and lack money. The Twelfth Street Branch Y. M. C. A., erected in 1912 in Hell's Bottom, has its boys' clubs and summer camp, Camp Lichtman; fosters dramatics, athletics, and forums; and attempts to aid employment. The Phyllis Wheatley Y. W. C. A., founded in 1905, aims at similar community service for women and girls, with Camp Clarissa Scott operating in the summer months. The Department of Playgrounds is coming to recognize the needs of this fourth of the city's population. Important playgrounds are the one at the historic Barry Farms, the Howard Playground, the Cardoza Playground, the Willow Tree Playground, Lincoln Playground, and the new Banneker Center. The 30 others are as crowded and active, and all are important. Community centers and settlement houses have programs of wide variety. In all of these, the paid Negro personnel is too small, and still underpaid.

Some other agencies in social welfare are the Washington Corps No. 2 of the Salvation Army and the fraternal organizations which launch occasional programs for civic betterment. Although the Police Boys' Clubs date back to 1933, plans for the inclusion of Negro boys in the surmised benefits are still in the making. The first lesson in civics for these boys seems to be their segregated status.

Athletics are, of course, popular. In the earlier years there was a strong governmental baseball league as well as many sand-lot teams. The present Washington Elite Giants, not indigenous like the old popular Le Droit Tigers, are successful in the National Negro League and therefore in good favor. Against such teams as the Pittsburgh Crawfords, the New York Black Yankees, the Homestead Grays, they put on colorful shows in the Griffith Stadium. Local basketball teams have become nationally known. Howard University and Miner Teachers College have heavy schedules in football and basketball against many of the best Negro collegiate teams, and the high schools are bitter athletic rivals. There are frequent track meets. Jesse Owens gave exhibitions at one of these. This was his only possible performance in Washington, as white colleges in the District do not allow Negroes to participate in their open meets. Tennis enthusiasts in Washington had a great deal to do with the founding of the American Tennis Association. Washington has had many Negro tennis champions, but with the paucity of the courts, public and private, tennis for a time declined. Negroes box in the District on "all-Negro cards." Negro golfers have only one inadequate golf course in the city. In spite of this, golf is increasing in popularity.

Baptists are the most numerous of the churchgoers in Washington; second to them are the Methodists, divided into several branches. There are churches of other denominations together with many independent store-front churches. The churches frequently have duplicated names, because of "splitting," or because of the shifting of population. Famous preachers of the early century were the Reverend George Lee, whose pulpit power was commensurate with his vast bulk, and the scholarly Reverend Walter Brooks and Reverend Francis Grimke. "Black Billy Sunday," the Reverend Alexander Willbanks, combined the resources of southern camp meetings with the tricks of his model. But even more spectacular have been the careers of Elder Solomon Lightfoot Michaux and Bishop "Daddy" Grace. The first of these, whose "Happy Am I" chorus and sermons are broadcast over Station WJSV, preaches to crowds in his Georgia Avenue tabernacle, with seats reserved for delegations of whites. Elder Michaux has experimented with communal ventures in lodging, and at present runs a One-Cent Cafe founded for him by Bernarr Macfadden. "Daddy" Grace, whose churches have swept from New Bedford to Augusta, Ga., has set up a House of Prayer at Sixth and M Streets NW. Store-front churches attract attention with crudely lettered signs, their unconscious humor checked by their patent sincerity. In one backward section a little church given over to noisy rousements and sing-song "gravy-giving" sermons is neighbor to a chapel of quiet, dignified services, pastored by a devoted and scholarly man who, without reaching a wide audience, has left a deep impress upon the community. That is a familiar contrast in the church life of Washington, and the less spectacular preachers who speak with quiet authority are not to be underestimated. Andrew Rankin Memorial Chapel at Howard University attracts some of the best known liberal preachers of both races, and the Howard University School of Religion aims to train a graduate ministry and to advance the admittedly backward condition of Negro preachers.

Out of more than $11,000,000 appropriated in 1936 to the public schools of the District of Columbia, approximately one-third was devoted to the colored schools. Education for Negroes in the District has come a long way from the first school founded by illiterate ex-slaves to the teachers' college, 3 senior high schools, 2 vocational schools, 6 junior high schools, and 40 elementary schools, with 1,004 teachers and 35,739 students. These schools are under the direction of Garnet C. Wilkinson, First Assistant Superintendent, divisions 10 to 13. Two other Negroes serve as second assistant superintendents, there is a Negro examining board and there is proportional membership on the Board of Education. The teaching force is unusually well prepared and the salaries are on the same scale as the salaries of the white teachers. The fact of segregation, however, must still be reckoned with. The theory of equal, though separate, accommodations breaks down into the fact of unequal facilities and equipment. Negro high schools are badly overcrowded and too often, instead of new structures, school buildings abandoned by whites are used for Negroes.

Howard University, called by some the "capstone of Negro education", is for the first time headed by a Negro, Dr. Mordecai W. Johnson. Under President Eugene Clark, Miner Teachers College, in spite of its youth, has received high rank from accrediting agencies. Frelinghuysen University, with Mrs. Anna J. Cooper as president, gives college instruction to students who must attend night classes. Miss Nannie Burroughs is the founder of the National Training School for Women and Girls, the school of the three B's: the Bible, the Bath, and the Broom, called the "nickel and dime school" because it depended for support almost wholly on contributions from Negroes who could not afford to give more.

Because of these universities there are many Negroes of ability in the humanities, and the social and natural sciences. Frequently their influence is greater than academic. At Howard University the *Journal of Negro Education* is ably edited. Carter G. Woodson edits the pioneering *Journal of Negro History* and directs the Association for the Study of Negro Life and History in this city. The weekly *Afro-American*, with a Washington edition, and the semiweekly Washington *Tribune* are the city's Negro newspapers, both tending to develop race consciousness.

These give some point to the boast of Washington's "cultural supremacy" among Negroes, but the boast is not too well founded. There is little literature even attempting to do justice to the facets of Negro life in Washington. There have been literary circles with a few poets, dramatists, and writers of fiction. The Little Theatre movement, initiated among Negroes by Alain Locke, editor of the *New Negro*, and Montgomery Gregory at Howard University, has only partially succeeded.

In 1903 the British Negro composer, Samuel Coleridge-Taylor, sponsored by a society named in his honor, conducted in Washington the first American performance of his *Hiawatha* trilogy. Other musical organizations of the century were the Clef Club and the Amphion Glee Club. The Washington Folk-Song Singers, directed by Will Marion Cook, presented as soloists Abbie Mitchell, Lottie Wallace, and Harry T. Burleigh, all later to become widely famed. The Washington Conservatory, under Mrs. Harriet Gibbs Marshall, was an important factor in musical education. Roland Hayes sang in Washington churches on his long, uphill road. Lillian Evans Tibbs, later known in opera as Madame Evanti, was one of Washington's well-known soloists. Of national popularity is the Howard University Glee Club under the direction of Roy W. Tibbs and Todd Duncan. The latter carried the role of "Porgy" in Gershwin's *Porgy and Bess*. Among jazz composers and orchestra leaders there are many Washingtonians; chief among these are Claude Hopkins and Duke Ellington, who has as one of his "hot" numbers, *The Washington Wabble*.

Although politically voluble, Negroes in Washington are still politically ineffectual. The hey-day of important political figures has passed. Oscar De Priest, Republican Congressman from Illinois, was followed by Arthur Mitchell, Democratic Congressman from the same State. There are still staunch Republicans and a Young Republican Club, and some of the old school have espoused the Liberty League; but there are many Democrats as well. The number of Negro appointees to administrative posts in the New Deal, while by no means adequate, is greater than in previous administrations. Many of these appointees are Washingtonians. Although political disquisitions may still stir the somnolence of barber shops, or break up friendships quadrennially, and although job-seekers abound, disfranchisement makes most of the Negroes politically apathetic. There is likewise a civic apathy. Civic organizations bringing grievances are often treated with scant courtesy by municipal authorities; without the vote they have little redress. There is a growing liberalism among Negroes who understand their plight, but the urging of such groups as the National Negro Congress and the N. A. A. C. P. too often meets with inertia and confusion. Segregation in Washington seems an accepted fact. Public buildings and public conveyances are not segregated, although on every southbound train Negro passengers are "jim-crowed." Negroes are not served in restaurants, saloons, hotels, movie-houses, and theaters, except those definitely set aside for them. Some stores will not accept their trade. Some governmental departments have separate accommodations, and some discriminate in the type of work offered to Negroes.

One boast, perhaps better founded than those of culture or civic status, is that Washington Negroes have a good time. Dances range in full plenty from the "house shouts" to the "bals masqués" of Washington's mythical Negro "400." Social scribes flatteringly speak of Negro "Mayfair" with no sense of incongruity. Social clubs are legion; the What-Good-Are-We Club (composed of ex-Howard students), is widely known for intensive hilarity. Though college sororities and fraternities seem to be awakening to social realities, their lavish "formals" are still the most important events on their schedules. Washington Negroes are great "joiners"; the largest orders are the Elks, Odd Fellows, Knights of Pythias, and the Masons, but some with an ancient history like "Love and Charity" linger on. The Musolit Club and the Capital City Pleasure Club have large memberships.

The movie-houses attract great crowds of Negroes. Of the chain theaters owned by the Lichtmans, three are located on U Street, the thoroughfare of Negro businesses and pleasure-seekers. The Howard Theater, something of a theatrical institution, affording both movies and fast-stepping, high-hearted shows, attracts an audience of both races. Poolrooms, short-lived cabarets, beer gardens, and eating places, from fried-fish "joints", barbecue, and hamburger stands to better-class restaurants, do an apparently thriving business. And yet, when the outsider stands upon U Street in the early hours of the evening and watches the crowds go by, togged out in finery, with jests upon their lips—this one rushing to the poolroom, this one seeking escape with Hoot Gibson, another to lose herself in Hollywood glamor, another in one of the many dance halls—he is likely to be unaware, as these people momentarily are, of aspects of life in Washington of graver import to the darker one-fourth. This vivacity, this gayety, may mask for a while, but the more drastic realities are omnipresent. Around the corner there may be a squalid slum with people jobless and desperate; the alert youngster, capable and well trained, may find on the morrow all employment closed to him. The Negro of Washington has no voice in government, is economically proscribed, and segregated nearly as rigidly as in the southern cities he contemns. He may blind himself with pleasure seeking, with a specious self-sufficiency, he may point with pride to the record of achievement over grave odds. But just as the past was not without its honor, so the present is not without bitterness.

In spite of the widespread segregation of the Negro in the District of Columbia, his story as told here has not concerned him solely. From the outset, white humanitarians have protested his enslavement and abuse, and farsighted statesmen have worked toward his integration in the total pattern. His schooling resulted from cooperation between Negroes and whites. Interracial organizations have worked toward an abolition of the injustices he faces. Governmental and municipal agencies have attempted to deal out to him a measure of what is his due. Today he is no longer asking, if he ever asked, to be considered as a ward. He asks to be considered as a citizen. But fulfillment of this hope seems still desperately remote.

BALLOU LIBRARY
BUENA VISTA COLLEGE
STORM LAKE, IOWA 50588
73105

The Negro has been donor as well as recipient. His contributions cannot be limited to those of menial or entertainer, as those who stereotype his character would insist. Many of the oldest inhabitants of the city who happen to be Negroes, and many newcomers, can boast of a record of citizenship as honorable as any. Culturally, the Negro has much to give, and, in spite of its being grudgingly received, has given much. No city can afford to disdain the creative potentialities of the Negro in music, drama, literature, and the arts. The scholars concentrated in Washington have a function greater than that of Negro scholars. They are American scholars who happen to be Negroes, and Washington and America have need of them. The Negro professional class of Washington, limited to service among Negroes, could contribute greatly to the advance of the entire city. The Negro has contributed. What could be a greater contribution is held in check by segregation.

From the preservation of the color-line in the District grave consequences arise. Educationally, segregation means the maintenance of a dual system—expensive not only in dollars and cents but also in its indoctrination of white children with a belief in their superiority and of Negro children with a belief in their inferiority, both equally false. Politically, it is believed by many that the determination to keep the Negro "in his place" has lessened the agitation for suffrage in the District. Economically, the presence of a large number of unemployed constitutes a critical relief problem; the low rate of pay received by Negro workers lowers the standard of living and threatens the trade-union movement. Socially, the effects of Negro ghettos are far-reaching. One cannot segregate disease and crime. In this border city, southern in so many respects, there is a denial of democracy, at times hypocritical and at times flagrant. Social compulsion forces many who would naturally be on the side of civic fairness into hopelessness and indifference. Washington has made steps in the direction of justice, but many steps remain to be taken for the sake of the underprivileged and for the sake of a greater Washington.